Expression of Hope:
THE MEL PENDER STORY

The story of gold medalist Melvin Pender:
The track world's black knight

Melvin Pender and Debbie Pender

ISBN 978-1-63525-111-1 (Paperback)
ISBN 978-1-63525-113-5 (Hard Cover)
ISBN 978-1-63525-112-8 (Digital)

Christian Faith Publishing, Inc.
296 Chestnut Street
Meadville, PA 16335
www.christianfaithpublishing.com

Printed in the United States of America

Contents

Dedication

I dedicate this book to my mother and my grandparents for giving me the inspiration and wherewithal to care for others and love all people. This is the family that taught me how to give, how to show respect for others, and how to receive God in my life which is the essence of my life.

Foreword

As told by Brigadier General Richard Dix

Many people were part of my journey to the rank of Brigadier General in the United States Army. I had many role models, my Uncle Sam Dix, who was a gunnery sergeant in the Marines, my godfather Willie Twilley, an enlisted man in the army, and Captain Melvin Pender was among them. Mel attended school with my father and uncles. He was a part of my journey to success, as were my grandparents, other relatives, teachers and coaches at Columbia High School in Decatur, Georgia and those at South Carolina State University, where I was enrolled in the No. 1 ranked Reserved Officers Training Corps program among colleges.

At the Brigadier General Promotion Ceremony where I was promoted in May of 2014, I wanted Captain Pender in the audience, along with one of my high school teachers, my high school and college coaches, family and friends. He came. He did not know that I wanted to publicly thank him and the others, for the impact they had on my life. As a small child growing up in Lynnwood Park, the second oldest African American community in the suburbs of Atlanta, every May we had the Lynnwood Park Day Parade. One year, I was maybe eight or nine years old, the grand marshal was Captain Melvin Pender of the 82nd Airborne Division. He was riding on a convertible, in full class A uniform, a maroon beret, with spit-shined jump boots! I was awestruck and immediately began to dream of becoming an officer in the United States Army and serve at Ft. Bragg, North Carolina, like my hero and Olympic gold medalist!

Mel had no idea what had transpired, but I believed that it was God's plan. I have fulfilled my dream and continue to serve our nation as many Lynnwood Park members before me! I have thanked Mel and the other Vietnam veterans before me, and I stand on their shoulders and proudly reach back to mentor the next generation!

The importance of role models should never be underestimated. Mel and I came from the same community in the Atlanta area. There is something to the adage that it takes a village to raise a child. As a soldier, Captain Pender was a symbol of hope for many young soldiers, and as an athlete he showed us all, that age is just a number, and he demonstrated what hard work and determination could do. I can identify with that. There were 3,400 officers under consideration for Brigadier General, and 34 were selected, of which I was one. I am truly honored, humbled and blessed to be serving and doing what I love. Hooah!

This gentleman you will read about was a combat soldier in the 82nd Airborne, served two tours of duty in Vietnam and made two different teams during the 1964 and 1968 Olympics as a sprinter. He was a gold medalist in 1968 on a record-setting relay team and he never forgot where he came from! A true blessing to all he meets!

Thank you Mel.
BG Richard B. Dix
Defense Logistics Agency Distribution Center

Preface

What type of spirit is it that we have, when fully connected, can actually rise up against all odds to soar? Not merely to walk or even run, but soar above the greatest of circumstances. To overcome all odds stacked against it to become that which it was meant to be!

What type of spirit, when given the opportunity, can rise not only once but multiple times, as much as needed to accomplish that which is set before it with fervency? Is it not this same spirit, when given its full potential, can slay the giants of misfortune and hate over coming with love and determination to be more than a conqueror? It is the spirit of greatness.

What fuels this spirit? What is its source of life? When fully awakened it is given the power to achieve that which is said to be impossible. Dreams become a reality and there is no stopping what has been put into motion.

This is the premise of which we tell the story of one American hero of whom his achievement and success has been driven by this spirit so great that we all possess; it is the spirit of man.

Acknowledgement

I am so grateful to Pete Scott Jr. who helped my wife and I complete this book. Pete too had been in the military and from there had an outstanding career with the Atlanta Journal Constitution. His expertise and knowledge of writing helped to polish and add just the right verbiage to make Expression of Hope a great read. Pete also grew up in Lynnwood Park which adds to a greater understanding of this wonderful community I have come from.

Introduction

My life has been a storybook of dreams that became reality. I know that there is a God, and he had a plan for me. I believe that he is still working on me. For several years, many of my friends have been telling me that I should write this book about my life-- but time goes so fast that you forget so many details of your life. When I look at all the things I have done, I sometimes wonder how I did all of them.

This book is being written as one of the chapters in American history that I hope our young people will read and try to understand that my life is one of the chapters of life that happened before 2015 and decades before there were twitter accounts, cellphones, the Internet, DVD players and iPads.

As part of the American dream, I hope young people will read and understand that all of us are experiencing life together. What one person does, rightly, or wrongly, will have an impact on the lives of many, and working to achieve success is possible, regardless of your life situation. I want everyone to see that no matter what you've done in your life, good, or bad, there is a higher power, in my case God, who is always with you if you believe and trust in Him, and he will see you through tough times, and good times, if you invite him into your lives.

I want my children, grandchildren, and their children, to read and know, that we all have a purpose in life, and that we should try to fulfill it by seeking the grace of God, relying on ourselves, our families, and well-meaning others. In the end, I hope those who read this book will understand that success requires hard work, making good decisions, dedication, and goal-setting. The road being traveled can be disappointing at times, rugged at times, lonely, and challenging, but in order to succeed there should be no mention of the words "I quit!"

Long after you read the last page of this book, it is my hope that like the taste of fine wine and great food, it will linger in your mind. My goal is that with anything I do, it is to perfection and perfection in this case would be that somehow my life's story will have changed yours. Whatever the life-task undertaken should be done with a goal in mind of being the best at what you are doing. May you be as blessed as I am and have been and may you find that dreams really do come true.

Chapter 1

Hope is Born

Now faith is the substance of things hoped for, the evidence of things not seen.

—Hebrew 11:1

Captain Melvin Pender!

"Please welcome the 1968 Olympics gold medalist Captain Melvin Pender Jr.," the booming voice of the emcee said in sounding out my name.

Whatever is intended for you in life is for you, and no one else. It will occur, one way or another. That was how I felt sitting and waiting for my name to be called at my recent induction into the Officers Candidate School Hall of Fame. It does not matter if you are cited in 2015, or years later; good things can, and will happen. Other officers, many outranking me, and cadets stood and cheered; it was indeed special. Some in attendance were family, but most were in the infantry like I was for two decades. Others held different military occupation specialties. We were all at the Infantry Museum at Fort Benning, Georgia, for induction into Officers Candidate School's Hall of Fame. For me, the event marked the tenth time I've been inducted into a Hall of Fame of some kind. Recently, the Georgia Military Veterans Hall of Fame bestowed a similar recognition, which was a great honor for me coming from my humble beginnings in Georgia. By the year 2016, I expect my picture and accomplishments noted, and hanging on the walls of the Floyd Building, which is a state building in Atlanta, for the public to view.

All of my Hall of Fame inductions have been tremendous. The OCS induction, however, seems to link together all my life experiences in and outside of the United States Army. I am honored by the recognition. The emcee for the evening reminded those in attendance of my service, two tours of combat duty during the Vietnam War, my service as a company commander in the 82nd Airborne Division, my work with then-ambassador William Colby, my receipt of the Bronze Star, and numerous other medals—it was uplifting. There was mention of how at the age of twenty-seven, I completed OCS and that I had competed in the 1964 Olympics in Tokyo as a sprinter. In addition, everyone learned how I was pulled out of combat in Vietnam in 1967 in order to compete in the 1968 Olympics in Mexico City, and earned a gold medal in the 4 x 100 meter relay. Although, I could not do it today, there was a mention that I still hold world records in the 50, 60, and 70-yard dashes. Once, they noted, I held the record in the 100-meter dash.

While recognizing my contributions in the military, and in the sports arena of track, my story will become very clear—the American dream is real, and I am living proof.

Throughout my life, using my convictions, faith, and perseverance, my dream has become a reality that I shall always embrace. It is my belief that I, Melvin Pender, am living the American dream because of the grace of God. I did not let my dream turn into a nightmare.

Both as a toddler in Dalton, Georgia, as well as my life as a youngster in the small suburban community of Atlanta called Lynwood Park, I wanted to be just like Audie Murphy. I watched his movie *To Hell and Back*, many times. I was often awestruck watching Murphy do heroic things. Then he was my hero. He was a military man and I wanted to be just like him. I even envisioned myself as a pilot. Murphy was like a living commercial for joining the army. It never dawned on me that the movie star was white, and I was black; he was just a soldier like I wanted to be, that's all.

For all intents and purposes, I felt like we were a lot alike. Audie Leon Murphy and I were small in stature. We both are just a few inches over five feet. I liked the idea of showing bigger people I could meet every challenge they put before me, and I could hold my own. He did too. He was a military man, and I wanted to become one—and I did, rising to the rank of captain. Murphy joined the army when he was eighteen. I got permission to join the Marine Reserves Program when I was fifteen, but later switched to the army at seventeen. This is America, I reasoned, and the military is one place where men and women often found they could win or lose their jobs based on their abilities. Like Murphy, I had won the love of my life back then, Robbie Nell Hood, got married, and became a father at the age of sixteen. Murphy was looking for a better life for himself and his family in Kingston, Texas, and I was doing something similar. He had a father who started a family of twelve, and his father disappeared; and mine started a family of two, I and my sister, Ann, and he left too. Our similarities, though, just about stopped there.

It never entered my mind then that there was a big difference in me and Audie Murphy. Again, I didn't think about the fact that he was white and I was black. Once President Harry S. Truman signed an executive order on July 26, 1948, mandating the military services become desegregated, I figured the sky was the limit for me in realizing my dream and that of others like me. Sadly, it was not until the Korean War of 1950–53, that the nation's leaders worked in earnest to eliminate segregation in the military. On October, 30, 1954, there was an official announcement from the Department of Defense that all the military was integrated. President Truman made it clear that he did not play, and he wanted the nation to understand fully that he wanted those of us who served our country to be treated fairly, and equally, in every aspect of military life.

Gone were the days when "Gold Star mothers" (a group of black mothers and wives of African American soldiers) faced poor treatment in America after they were invited by France to honor the

430 black soldiers who died on French soil in World War I. However, despite the president's declaration and the support the policy handed down through the years within the military, I faced, and conquered, many challenges of race in the effort to reach my goal of "being somebody."

Daring to Dream

Overall, I am just a country boy at heart. One of my favorite sandwiches is still bologna, lettuce, and tomato, with mayonnaise. I've tried fancy world cuisine, but I still like bologna, lettuce, and tomato. I was born at a time when life was much simpler, when we didn't have a lot and we didn't know the difference. I was born when we had to use our imagination a whole lot and our happiness was not dependent upon material things. It was a time when many dreams seemed impossible to achieve and our desires to be all that we could be and make great names for ourselves was more of a fantasy than a reality. Still, we dreamed big dreams of fame and fortune, and I certainly could almost touch and taste my success. I was determined, even desperate, to be somebody.

As a preteen, I had no idea how I would achieve my goal, but I would keep pushing against the limitations that society and circumstances had imposed on me. I was determined. From my earliest childhood memories, I realize now that I was driven.

Frequently, at this time in my life, now that I am in my seventies, I often find myself reflecting about "back in the day," in talking about the times that I have lived, loved, and labored through life. A time of phenomenal transitions and changes that have remolded and reshaped the world. Now, some of the fantasies and dreams of many in this country have become realities. An African American occupies the highest elective office in the land, president of the United States of America. It pays to dream big. In my own way, I have proven the truth of this statement, over and over again.

As I revisit the country roads and highways, the twists and turns, the ups and downs of my life's journey, it is my hope that through my life experiences, someone will catch a glimpse of the inspiration, motivation, and fuel that helped to drive my life. The struggles, pain, achievements, and wisdom I have gained through the years are the things I would like to share with everyone, especially a younger generation that often feels disenfranchised, deprived, and desperate. I hope young people of this generation will embrace the biggest dreams possible, even if they are discounted as fantasies by others.

Grady Baby

Picture of Mama, Ann and me

First, let me say with pride, I am a Grady baby! Henry Grady Memorial Hospital is named for a famous journalist from the South, and there is a school of journalism at the University of Georgia that bears his name. Grady is located in Atlanta, Georgia. Being born at Grady is a kind of status symbol that you are indeed an Atlantan, if you say you are. Unlike now, Grady was segregated, with very little space and equally meager services to offer the black population of the area. It was on Halloween, October 31, 1937, that Mr. and Mrs. Melvin Pender Sr. proudly welcomed the birth of their son, Melvin Pender Jr., who, together with his sister, Ann, would be the only children of the family. At that time, Atlanta was "the country," strictly rural, nothing like the international metropolitan area it has become today. There were trees, woods, pastures, fields, farms, dairies, and other agricultural offerings where major interstates, I-285, I-75, I-20, now are used to allow residents to work, shop and play at malls, corporate skyscrapers, and hotels that dominate the area. But for humble country folks, such as we were, there was a certain fame attached to being a "Grady" baby. Any mark of distinction, however tenuous, was greedily, almost gratefully, grasped by black people in those days. We lived in a South that treated black people as less than human, a South heavily scarred by the ugliness of segregation practiced in all areas of life, from the cradle to the grave.

I am proud to say that although many new buildings have been added to the Grady hospital over the years, the part where I was born still stands today. It is not segregated.

My parents lived in the Sandy Springs area, about twenty to thirty-five minutes away from the hospital. They lived in what was called a shotgun house. That is a house with so many holes that you could see straight through from front to rear. There was no such thing as insulation, and the gaps between the wall boards allowed you to see through the house while standing outside. The roads leading to and from our homes, throughout the whole neighborhood, were red Georgia clay. They were very slick and muddy when it rained. Pine trees and oak trees seemed to be everywhere, but I don't remember them falling that much like they do today. There were man-sized potholes everywhere, and many times, the few cars that came in and through the neighborhood would get stuck in the mud. Whenever this happened, there would be great excitement, especially from the children. Everyone would come out of their homes to lend their help, and pure brute force, to get the travelers out and on their way.

At the time of my birth, my mother was twenty, and my father was twenty-two years old. My sister, Ann, had just come into the world the year before on January 6, 1936. She was born in Dalton. Both Daddy and Momma were from Dalton. It is a small town that was known for its bedspread mills. The mills were major employers of black people in the community. Dalton was a safe place to live, and as long as everyone knew their place, there was tranquility in the community. Today, Dalton is known for its carpet mills, which attract purchasers from all over the world.

My parents moved to Sandy Springs with my mother's parents so Momma could have me at Grady Hospital. My father, Melvin Sr., had a 1935 Ford car that barely ran, but it got the family to our new home. Eventually, it even got my mother, Evelyn, to Grady hospital just fine when it was time for my birth. After I was born, my family returned to live in Dalton. My father was a real hard worker, and a hustler. He was funny, and everyone liked him, which was a great asset to a hustler. Although I was a little boy, I can remember him selling corn liquor to make ends meet. I also remember being only about three years old when the police came to our house. I was in my nightshirt and it hung down long on me. Daddy had me sit on a five-gallon jug during the whole time the police were there. My shirt covered it up, and I saved the day. That was the talk of the year, and I never got tired of hearing that story as it was embellished and repeated as getting one over on the authorities.

My dad did what he had to do to provide for us. That was just the way it was back then. That is what a real man did then, whatever it took to survive and support your family.

Like most of the people in my Dalton neighborhood, we were poor but did not know it. Momma worked as a maid, cleaning and cooking for rich white people. We had plenty of food and clean clothes to wear. It seemed as if we were not lacking anything. The Pender family was well-known and very popular in Dalton. Momma had a hard time keeping up with Daddy though. Like all the Pender men in Dalton, women were very attracted to Daddy. The Pender men had a reputation of being "ladies' men." Even though my dad loved my mother very much, he was influenced by his brothers and cousins who were young, wild, and drinkers. Their ways, and his, led much to my mother's heartache.

Chapter 2

On the Move Again

Our next move was to Chicago. I was around four years old. It was wartime and there was a lot of work to be found in the factories there. Momma worked for the government building airplanes for the war, and Daddy was doing the same. It was in 1942 that I experience one of the saddest days in my life. I was only five years old, and my sister, Ann was six, when my father was drafted. He went into the navy. When he left, I thought I would never see him again. It was devastating to me as a young boy who loved his father very much. As I watched him leave, I fretted that he might never come back alive.

After my dad left, Momma took Ann and me back to Atlanta to live with her parents: Grandmother Rosa, we called Wowa, and our Grandfather William, we called Grandpa. Everyone else called him Will. Momma went back to Chicago to continue working for the government. Wowa was working as a maid for a rich family and lived in the quarters alongside the main house that was built for servants. The house we occupied was small, and Ann and I had to share a room. There was no bathtub, so our baths were taken in a large, number 9 round tin tub. There was no central heating, so it was my job to bring the coal in from under the house to burn it for heating. We had three stoves. One was in the living room to heat the main part of the house, one in the kitchen for cooking, and one in our bedroom.

My grandparents were the greatest! Grandmother was a very sweet woman who loved my sister and me very much. She could cook and was known for her pies. My grandfather was a hard worker who worked at Ervindale Dairy for thirty years. He was a very patient and wise man. I attribute the positive aspects of my character today to the love, guidance, and wisdom of my grandparents. Both of them worked very hard all their lives. Grandpa had only a third-grade education but his knowledge, wisdom, and understanding of life had been hard won by the lessons of a harsh society and an even tougher life. Today, one might think of someone having only a third-grade education as not being very bright, but to the contrary, he was very intelligent. He was a self-taught man who loved to pass on his knowledge as well as encouraging the importance of bettering one's self through education and learning. He always had time for Ann and me. There were many things that my grandfather taught me, but the greatest thing he passed on to me was the ability to "listen and learn." I can still hear him saying to me, "Listen...If you really listen, you will learn so much." It is a lesson that I have tried to pass on in my life, especially when I have the opportunity to speak with young people.

Momma returned from Chicago about a year after Ann and I did. She had earned enough money, with the help of Daddy's military pay, to buy a house in Dalton. It was a little house with a tin roof. I loved to hear the sound of the rain on that roof. I was six and had to be the little man since my father was not around. I learned to wash and iron my clothes, starching my shirts with Argo starch and pressing my jeans with creases down the legs. My shoes were shined and kept good for school. I was always a neat child. Mama said that I was always cleaning and trying to help her out around the house. I took my new responsibilities seriously. I wanted my father to be proud of me whenever he returned. I prayed it would happen real soon.

Patriotism

Adults can teach patriotism, but sometimes, as children, you just learn it based on what's going on around you in the world. That's the way I got mine, and it has not left me. I recall when I was about seven years old, I was highly inspired to do my part for my country. We were in the throes of World War II. When we went to the movies or listened to the radio, we heard about the war.

Because my mama worked in Chicago to support the war and my daddy was in the navy, I felt I had a part to play too. Well, there was a man in our neighborhood who was about four feet eleven inches tall, and we only knew him by his nickname of Shorty.

He made his living by collecting scrap iron. He had a big truck with extended sides, and he used the truck to collect scrap iron for the military. Every week we would see Shorty come through our neighborhood picking up a load. My buddies Jimmy Toliver, Sonny Mann, Henry Austin and I got together and decided that we could show our patriotism too and make some money for ourselves.

We took wagons, put sides on them like Mr. Shorty's truck and combed the community for small scrap iron. Then when Mr. Shorty would come around, we would sell what we collected to him. We always made sure that we got at least $2 so that each of us would get fifty cents. It was just enough for us to go to the movies, have a hot dog and Coke, and still have twenty-cents left in our pockets.

When we realized what we were doing, we began collecting empty milk bottles and soda bottles from the Nehi grape, Coke, and other sodas we had then. Each bottle brought in one cent, a penny, and we all set as our goal raising at least ten cents a piece. I didn't realize it then, but I guess that's where my business acumen first began. We prided ourselves as being patriotic because we were following the steps of Mr. Shorty.

Patriotism remained the order of the day. We exercised it in the schools; we always began our day with the Pledge of Allegiance to our country. It was emphasized in our churches, at the barber shop, and at corner stores. The thing about Dalton back then was that we were not as segregated as other areas in the South. White and black lived comfortably near each other, and when things happened to disrupt our community we pulled together to support one another. The war was no exception to our rule; we all pulled together to support the war effort.

You would not know it by the way some talk about veterans, but according to military officials of more than 2.5 million blacks who registered for the draft in World War II, about 909,000 served in the army, approximately 167,000 were in the navy with my father, and over 17,000 blacks enlisted in the Marine Corps.

After two years away, my father came home safe and sound from the war. He went to work in the bedspread factories cleaning their machines at night and getting them ready for the next day's work. He would take me sometimes to help out. I could tell that he didn't like doing that type of work because he had held better positions working in Chicago where he also made more money. Even so, I learned about work ethics during the time I spent with my dad. Back in those days, most families had a man in the house. It was an environment and a time when everyone worked hard, and we thought nothing of it. Families pulled together to make ends meet. Unfortunately, my mother and father were having a difficult time making a go of their marriage. He had come back from the war very unsettled and developed a drinking problem. All this led to a lot of fussing and fighting between them. Within a year they were divorced. Once again, my father was gone, returning to Chicago to restart his life. Again I was devastated. I know that divorce is painful for everyone in the family, but I was sure that there was no hurt as great as my own.

Divorce was not as common in my community as it is today. I wanted my father to stay with me and for us to be a family. The whole thing was hard for me to understand since all my other friends had their fathers at home. I felt then that I probably would never see him again. It seemed he was gone for good. So, I resorted back to my role as the man of the family and resolved to be all that I had wanted my father to be.

Returning to Dalton at the end of one of my summer vacations with my father in Chicago, I accepted the hard truth. I knew I had to grow up on my own. I had to accept that my father would not be there for me in the way I wanted, or had prayed. I was now on my own.

Good Visions Emerged

My elementary school in Dalton, GA

My desire to be responsible did not eliminate nor diminish the simple pleasures of childhood. I took on the role I felt I had to, and I took my duties seriously. Besides, my mom did not play when it came to chores. She was strict and made sure that we got our work done and done right. It was when I was finished with my chores that you would find me outside playing hard with my friends. I developed friendships during that time that I have kept for life. One such friend is Walter Miller. We spent many weekends together. I remember when we made noise at night that Walter's father, a tough man, would come in with his belt and slap our covers. He knew how to get our attention and get us to sleep. My other friends were Jimmy Tolliver, Sonny Cobb, Bucky Rogers, Joe Brooks, John Shepard, and my cousin Henry Austin. This was the gang. Now, when we said "the gang," it was not like the gangs of today. It just meant that we were a group of friends who loved each other like brothers. We hung out together after we had all completed our chores, engaged in boyish mischief, and had lots of fun. We knew one another's families as well as we knew our own, and we all looked out for each other. We played hard and used our imagination and ingenuity, building go-carts out of any pieces of scrap we could find. There was nothing to compare with shooting marbles with the boys or riding our bikes all over Dalton. Not to mention playing superheroes. Yes, we had them too. Our favorites were cowboys and Indians and, of course, Superman. All these things stirred our imaginations and inspired flights of fantasy as we vowed to be heroes when we grew up. We would constantly compete against each other while having lots of fun all at the same time. Baseball and running races were some of our endeavors, and even though I was the smallest of the guys, I managed to be the fastest. That led to my popularity, and so I was the one that everyone wanted to have on their team or to beat.

Cub Scouts

In addition to the usual games and pastimes that occupied the neighborhood children, joining the Cub Scouts provided a defining moment in my life. Mr. Willis, a distant cousin of mine (who is now deceased), had the task of doing something special for the black kids in Dalton. He wanted them to have some of the same experiences that white kids shared. When he returned from serving in WWII as a marine, he started his own funeral home and also started the first African American Cub Scout troop in the area. We loved it. It was one of the many experiences that helped to shape my life. On one very important assignment in earning our merit badges, we had to find a lost boy on the mountain. Mr. Willis staged the event on one of the mountains around Dalton, and it was our job to find him. We knew that this was perhaps the most important thing we had ever had to accomplish in our young lives. This was also the first time that we were paired up with the other white troops in the area. Remember, segregation was still the way of life in the South. We worked together searching out every rock formation, looking around trees, in bushes, until we reached the mountaintop. The climb up the mountain and the excitement of searching for the lost child was a very rewarding experience. It was the first time that black and white children in Dalton worked together for the important cause of saving a boy's life. It was only when we got to the top of the mountain that we learned that it was not in fact a real boy but rather a mannequin. I do not know if we were happy or relieved, but it was a valuable, lasting experience that made a very strong impression on me. It was at this time that I began to think more and more that I would like to join the United States Marines like Mr. Willis. We celebrated together on top of the mountain with hot dogs and Coca-Cola, not as separate units, white and black, but as one. On that day, there was no color, just kids.

A First Crush

There were many other great moments during my young days growing up in Dalton, and pretty girls too. I was in the fourth grade when I really noticed girls existed. One such girl was Barbara Mann, on whom I had a major crush. Let me tell you about her. I thought Barbara was the prettiest little thing that I had ever set eyes on. She was from New York, and every summer since I could remember, she would come down to visit her grandma and cousins. Now, the way I always found out that Barbara was in town was through Kathleen, my classmate. There were only four phones in our neighborhood, and we didn't have one. However, Kathleen was a very reliable source of information. She knew I liked Barbara and would make it her duty to tell me when she had arrived in town. She was pretty. She had a great smile, naturally long hair, and it was even more beautiful when she smiled just at me. Her presence would mark the beginning of my summer. When she left to return home to New York, much of my summer ended too. Over time, I did not see her anymore and that was that.

My budding relationship with Barbara did not always go smoothly. Two painful memories come to mind. Barbara and I were out in the church parking lot after church services one Sunday, and I accidentally slammed her finger in the car door. I felt so bad about it, and thought I had broken it. Fortunately, that did not spoil our friendship. There was another instance that I recall vividly. Barbara was over at my friend Kathleen's house. It was at night, and I wanted to see her, and so my friend, Raleigh Spriles, and I got on our bikes and rode over there. We were frightened by the unexpected appearance of Kathleen's father. Initially, her dad was not at home when we got there. So once we became aware he was home, we jumped on our bikes and sped off. Well, after a while, I noticed that Raleigh wasn't with me. I backtracked calling for him.

"Raleigh! Raleigh!" I yelled almost in a panic.

"I'm in the tar branch. I'm in the tar branch!" he repeated.

I don't know where that tar branch came from, but Dalton had at least four or five of them. They were big holes, and instead of water resembling a pond, there was tar. Raleigh and his bike had both landed in the tar branch that was almost waist high. He was able to stand up, but he could not move, I had to pull and pull until I got Raleigh and his bike out. We have laughed about this for years.

Almost on My Own

In rural or urban settings, there always seemed to be something memorable about summers, both good and bad. Well, the same summer my crush was magnified with Barbara, my world was crushed by the reality that my dad really didn't know how to be the father I saw with a lot of my friends.

I wanted my dad with me to do fun things with me like go to baseball games and fishing—things kids in my community did with their dads, things I had seen in the movies. I had his love, which he demonstrated in giving me gifts, but I didn't have his time. I felt this loss very deeply. I would rather have had time with him than all the gifts in the world. Even though I loved my mother very much, I continually missed my father. My days were sad without my dad. Sometimes, I could be having fun with my friends but still feel the sadness of missing my father. I often dreamed about him, longing for the days we had together, wishing that I could go back in time, and that those days would never come to an end. When I was ten years old, I got very angry with my mother. I do not recall the reason, but I told her that I was going to run away and go live with my father. My mother was very upset. She called my father, and he agreed to let me go and stay with him, so I was sent by train to Chicago for the summer. Old people always tell you to be careful what you wish for, sometimes you'll get more than you bargained for, and I did.

I spent a lot of time with my dad while he drove a cab. His cab was known as a Jitney Cab and he covered the South Park area, which is now Martin Luther King Jr. However, my father took business wherever he could and would end up driving all over Chicago. I learned my way around the city riding around with him, and today I can still navigate my way all over Chicago. Dad was a very sharp dresser and always had pretty girlfriends. During this time, he had gotten married again to a beautiful woman named Ines. Miss Ines was kind and gracious. She was biracial of black and white. Daddy drank a lot and didn't come home until one or two in the mornings. I knew Miss Ines was getting tired of it, and I had a strong feeling it would only be a matter of time that she too would leave my father.

Looking back, I guess the fact that he didn't have his own father around him meant he never knew how to be otherwise and never figured it out for himself either. Back in his day, the men worked out in the fields. They labored long, hard days for the white families that employed them at a pittance and didn't have much time for their families.

No matter what was happening in my life with my dad, I wanted to make my mother proud of me. Making my mother proud soon became my main goal in life. It was very important. In my thinking, I had concluded that my father had deserted us. It was therefore up to me to look out for my mother and sister and to bring honor to our family. If I could become somebody important, then that would satisfy the longing that I felt driving me on the inside. With limited resources available to me, and even fewer opportunities that would allow me to become the kind of man I so longed to be, I was constantly looking for a way forward. Finally, it was a train that came through our town filled with black soldiers that renewed my interest of joining the army. The trains would come through our town, the black soldiers on one end of the train and the white soldiers on the other end. I would ask my momma *why*? Why can't they ride together? My mother's reply was, "I don't know, but someday it will happen." The black soldiers would throw games and money to us. I was a Cub Scout, and I just loved uniforms. Momma bought me both a navy and an army suit, and I was so proud to wear either one of them. Secretly, there was another reason that I loved them. In my uniform, I felt like my daddy, and somehow felt closer to him even though he wasn't there.

My youthful admiration for Audie Murphy heightened because the war consumed our airways. It was wartime, and much of what we saw was about joining up, doing our duty to the country where we lived, and becoming a hero. When I went to the movies, I would see Murphy and his success in WWII. He was our superhero of the day and inspired many of us young boys to go and serve our country.

Airplanes always held a fascination for me. I would watch until they were out of sight, whenever they flew over. Plane travel was not that common back in the day, so to see an airplane was exciting. How could it stay up in the sky and travel at such speed at which it traveled occupied my mind for hours on end. I thought it would be the greatest thing to be a pilot. Often, I would fantasize about piloting a plane myself, up among the clouds, reaching closer to heaven. I had never heard of any black pilots, but that never stopped me from seeing myself flying high.

There was no mention of Eugene Jacques Bullard until 1994. He was well-known in France, but it was not until former Georgia Governor Zell Miller declared October 9, 1994, as his day in Georgia. Bullard was recognized as the world's first black fighter pilot in World War I. He was from Georgia. He was a boxer for a while and worked his way to France. He became a pilot in the French Foreign Legion and the LaFayette Flying Corps. Back then, because of his race, he was barred from doing the same thing in the United States. The albatross of racism in our past has hurt our country so bad. Just imagine what Bullard and others could have done for the good of this country if their dreams could have been realized. I was aware of the Tuskegee Airmen, and I give honor to them; they broke the color barriers of flight in this country.

"Suitcase" Simpson

Young men will always dream, and I was full of them. Becoming great, being recognized by everyone was one of mine. I wondered what it would be like to be the greatest at something. How about being a great athlete? I thought. I did not know of many black men who were famous as athletes, yet it was still a dream of mine. I had not heard of sprinter Jesse Owens, in fact I could identify with only one famous person, and he was a cousin from Dalton, Georgia. Our country had conditioned African Americans to think so little of themselves, even I could not appreciate his stature in life. His name was Harry Leon "Suitcase" Simpson. His nickname in Dalton was Goody, because he ran errands for other people and did not hesitate to help anyone in Dalton. National sportswriters derisively called him Suitcase because at six feet one inch and 180 pounds, he wore a size 13 shoe, which was uncommon then, and they jokingly said he had feet as large as a suitcase.

Harry became a famous baseball player in the old Negro League who had made it to the major leagues in 1951–53 with the Cleveland Indians. He also played for championship teams of the New York Yankees and the Chicago White Sox in the 1950s. He was one of the first black men to integrate baseball in the American League. He was with the Yankees when they lost in the World Series in 1957 and when they won it in 1958. He was a first baseman and outfielder for teams in Kansas City, Chicago, and Pittsburgh, and his teammates included such stars as Roger Maris, Roberto Clemente, Bill Virdon, and William Stanley "Bill" Mazeroski. Simpson was twenty-five when he began his professional baseball career and died in 1979 and is buried at the West Hill Cemetery in Dalton.

No matter where my family landed, there always seemed to be something that kept linking me to what I wanted to do in life.

Chapter 3

Visiting Wowa

My family tried to make a home in Dalton, but looking back, it had to be destiny that brought us back to Lynwood Park in 1949. My father had returned and left again. Mama, Ann, and I moved to a small, all-black, single-family home community in North Atlanta. I had just completed the sixth grade. We moved into the home that my grandfather built. It was built out of scrap material, anything he could get his hands on, and put together by relatives and neighbors. But it was theirs, and they called it home. We did too. This house had no running water or indoor plumbing. That did not come until later. Ann and I shared a room. We were happy to be back with Wowa and Grandpa; they loved us so much.

As I mentioned earlier, Wowa was such a great cook. Her sweet potato pie and pound cake were the absolute best. Because Grandpa worked at the dairy, he would bring fresh milk home daily, and Wowa would stay busy churning butter for the next day's breakfast. Ann and I thought they were rich. We didn't know any difference. Food was plentiful, and we were always dressed nicely, and that was good enough for us. When we were living in Dalton, it was always exciting for us to go visit her and stay overnight. Wowa had two pigs and a chicken coop from which we had fresh chicken for dinner sometimes. They said the pigs were Ann's and mine, but really one day, they too would be eaten for many good meals.

Wowa kept a vegetable garden and was always in the kitchen making pies; you could smell them when you drove up in the driveway. My favorite was sweet potato pie and peach cobbler. We had peach and fig trees all around her place, and blackberries too. I would go out and pick the fruit and bring it to Wowa. She knew what to do with it. Now, Ann wasn't too fond of picking blackberries since they had a tendency to carry red bugs, or chiggers, as many people know them. They would get all over you, and then you had troubles. So to avoid that, Ann left the picking to me. I got the job of gathering eggs from the chicken coop and then we would have the greatest breakfasts. On Sundays before church, Wowa was up early fixing us a huge spread. Sometimes it was chicken smothered in gravy and at other times eggs and pork chops, but always there were biscuits. We ate good, played hard, and learned valuable lessons of life while in the care of Wowa and Grandpa, and I always wanted to be there.

The "Sub"

Our family home in Lynwood Park

Lynwood Park is a community located about twenty minutes north of downtown Atlanta. We knew it as a subdivision of Atlanta, thus the nickname the Sub. It was looked upon by us as part of Atlanta, even though it was in the northern part of the suburb and DeKalb County. At one time, it even had its own city council and was called North Atlanta. I don't know what changed things. I know one of our residents, Deacon Luke Holsey, was on it. Mr. Holsey lived to be over one hundred years, and was well respected. Today, most of the modest one-story homes I knew as a youngster have been torn down by developers and replaced with massive three-story mini mansions with price tags that exceed $600,000 and some in excess of $1 million in what is now part of the City of Brookhaven. It is a developer's paradise.

Back in my day, it was our humble neighborhood. Everyone knew everyone, and everyone looked out for each other. We were a tight-knit group of families. There wasn't a thing that happened that everyone didn't hear or know something about it. In many ways, Lynwood Park was kind of a meshing of the mythical Mayberry RFD from television, and Harlem, New York, all rolled into one.

Like Dalton, Lynwood Park had its share of role model families, some who stressed education as a way to success: pastors who worked to guide our conduct and creative people who were talented singers and other kind of artists and great cooks! There was even a sewing circle club.

On Saturday nights, you could walk outside your home and the aroma of collard greens, green beans, fried chicken, cakes, and pies filled the air as some of the best cooks ever were cooking. It does not take much imagination for me to remember the flaky, soft taste of paper-sack brown, cathead biscuits like the ones I used to get from Mrs. Idell Jones, my friend Columbus' mother. The biscuits were a big part of my hang outs with Columbus and his brother, Wallace.

Decades ago, there were more than a thousand African American residents of Lynwood Park. Now, gentrification has transformed my old community into one that is predominantly white, with about seventy to two hundred black families remaining. Just about all of the churches remain, but their memberships are declining. One church, Little Zion Missionary Baptist Church, now has a black and white congregation.

Over 100 years ago residents came from all over Georgia to make their home in Lynwood Park. So, as a boy growing up there life was different. It was a place where almost everyone knew everyone; whether it was good bad or indifferent they stuck together. Most of the streets in Lynwood Park were not paved in the 1950s, and sidewalks did not exist when I was growing up. I often used the sidewalk space in front of my house and many of my neighbors to practice playing golf. Most of what I did was putting.

As a teenager, we did not have anything like what is available to young people now. A military veteran used to show movies at one of the churches to provide an entertainment outlet. There were three barbershops, one was operated by a woman, Mildred "Mook" Jackson. She was my friend Robert Jackson's aunt and the one who cut my hair. There were three main cabbies in the community:

Mr. Turner was the most popular of them all. He was a disabled veteran who did not have use of his legs. He had his cab modified so that he could operate the pedal, brakes, gears, and everything with his hands. He did a booming business. His old charcoal-gray car still sits in the driveway at the home of his widow on Windsor Park across from the Lynwood Park Church of God in Christ. We needed the cabbies because the bus line nearest to our community was about three to five miles away.

There were two nightspots (we called them juke joints); one was a club on the corner entering the community at Osborne Road and House Road (now Windsor Parkway). It had several pool tables in it, modest foodstuffs like hamburgers, a jukebox and room to dance; also there were girls. There was one main grocery, Danneman's, and two smaller ones operated by Ms. Gertrude Pitts. Her nephew, Judge Marvin Arrington, once was vice mayor of the City of Atlanta. The other store in the community was Miss Lackey's on Victoria Avenue.

We had some local celebrities to make their way through Lynwood Park too. Among the achievers are Dr. Theodore Allen, a dentist, a popular entertainer named Lotsapapa, because of his huge size, and a near-blind Albino piano player called Piano Red had relatives in my community as well. Gladys Knight and the Pips were frequent visitors in our community, even though they did not live there. Most residents were just plain folks—overall, good folks. Some have stood out. Nowadays, some other celebrities with ties to Lynwood Park are international comedian George Wallace and offensive lineman Steve Wallace (who won more than one Super Bowl ring as a member of the San Francisco 49ers), and Army General Richard Dix.

Many of the residents helped me to shape my life and had an influence making me into the man I am today. First, there was the late Mrs. Idell (Jones). Just like so many black people back then, Mrs. Idell was a very special woman. She was strong and tough. She did not let anything slip by her. At her mailbox every morning, she would stand and watch out for all the children walking down Osborne Road to our only school. It did not matter that she was in her house slippers, dressed any way she wanted, and peering at you over the glasses she wore, with snuff in her bottom lip; you would have to pass by her, and it seemed that she kept record of who went by that day and who didn't walk down Osborne Road, the main route to the school. If she didn't see you, she would phone the school, and your mother. If anyone was just plain being truant, you were not just in double trouble, it was triple jeopardy. The schoolteacher got you, your mother got you, and most of all, Mrs. Idell got you. After one experience, you never wanted to skip school again in your life.

People like Mrs. Idell were part of the backbone of our community. They helped kids like me maintain good conduct. I didn't have a choice, really. The adage about "it takes a village to raise a child," easily could have come from Lynwood Park.

Mrs. Idell loved to watch us play baseball.

"Hit the ball, Junior!" she often shouted at me.

I would hate for her to call me Junior, since I didn't want to represent my father, but I owe so much to Mrs. Idell for her support. That's why I say that she is one of the reasons I try to pay my blessing from her forward, when it comes to giving back to our young people. I was best friends with her son, Columbus, and as such, was always treated as a part of the family. So naturally, it followed that I went to church with them. When Sunday morning came around, we made our way in Mr. Wallace's car to Zion Baptist Church in Chamblee, Georgia. This was a good-sized church of about one hundred people located about twenty minutes from Lynwood Park. I loved going to the church. It was very family-oriented, and there was a real sense of belonging. After church, we rushed home, donned our uniforms, and hit the field for baseball. The whole community came out to watch. Our field was called the Hole since it was in a ravine. Water from the rain ran off into it, causing holes to form in the field. The men would take out their trucks and drag it to fill the holes.

Sunday afternoon was baseball time in Lynwood Park. Preachers had good sense not to hold church too long, and they too seemed to really like the idea of praising the Lord in the morning and getting families together in the day to watch baseball games too. Our baseball team was called the Lynwood Tigers, and my position was shortstop. Catching the ball was no problem for me, and I could hit it just fine; however, it was the throwing that I had problems with since the ball never went straight. I was the shortest and youngest on the team; they couldn't get a uniform for me, so I wore a white T-shirt and jeans. Our coach, Mr. Wallace Jones, was Mrs. Idell's husband. She was very involved with the team and was more than just our cheering section.

Mrs. Idell's other major contribution to our baseball games was to make the best "fiss sandwiches" as we called them. They consisted of croaker or mullet fish, two pieces of "lite" (white) bread, hot sauce, and mustard. She had many customers. After playing hard, we all looked forward to biting into her hot spicy sandwiches. Mrs. Idell loved to fish, and I would often go fishing with her and Columbus. Our fishing was done in a muddy hole near our house. We'd get up early in the morning, go down to that muddy hole, and come home later in the day with our catch.

We had some great young athletes on our baseball team, and I believe that some of those kids could have grown up and played major league baseball if they had been given the chance to try out for the big teams. Carl Volen, my other best friend, was Mrs. Idell's nephew. He moved from Washington DC to live with Mrs. Idell and her family. Carl and I quickly became friends since we were about the same size and age. We were both very competitive and loved to challenge each other. Carl was an excellent baseball player, one you could really count on. He had an offer to go play professional baseball, but like me, he was told he was just too small. Later on, we had one young man, Larry Cantrell, drafted by the Cleveland Indians, but he died without getting a chance at a spot on a pro team.

Another community activity that was enjoyable growing up was swimming. We had a place to swim, but it was not what one would ordinarily think of as a pool. Rather, it was another mudhole. Silver Lake was nearby, located in the nearby all-white neighborhood. We swam there for a while although we were not supposed to do this back then. However, when my very good friend, Bobby, drowned, that ended our swimming in the lake. We settled for the safety of our own neighborhood mudhole slash swimming pool.

Our school's football team reflected the impoverishment of our community and we only played about five other teams. However, that did not discourage our community. They came out every time and cheered us on wholeheartedly. There was a strong cohesive feeling in Lynwood Park—a strength that came from being together on so many issues. This feeling stayed with me throughout my years of schooling in Atlanta. It was also that sense of home that I looked forward to, many years later, when I came home on leave, or from my many travels.

Let me pause here a minute. Almost all of the football teams back then were about evenly matched. One of my old classmates believe some of our team members, who once attended school, but might not have always been enrolled during a given school year, often became team members as the bus would pull out of the community headed for a game. Somehow, we always managed to have extra uniforms that fit, and they played. I don't really remember that, but I do remember having teammates like Raymond Parks, Matthew "Plug" Moore, Clyde "Goober" Blake, John "Tippy" Summerour, Robert "Sonny" Jackson, Bobby Jett, Freddie Julian, Tompy Truitt, and Coot Julian forming a big line in front of quarterback Columbus "Loud Wire" Jones, and Ralph "Zeke" Daniels, while Wilmer "Lil Hal" Harris, Carl Volen, and I carried the ball in the backfield.

Back in my old neighborhood of Lynwood Park, track was something we never had at school. We did football but not track (baseball was our community team). My old principal, Professor L. A. Robinson, who doubled as our coach, Scout leader, and the extracurricular activities man at our small school, wasn't able to provide the other sports. The main reason I suppose we didn't attempt it is we never had an area on which to practice. Back then, we practiced football and baseball, on a red clay dirt area filled with rocks (usually, no rocks smaller than marbles) and some as big as a fist. We had to avoid them as best we could. No one wanted to get tackled or knocked down.

All my life, I knew I could run because I was a pretty fast halfback in football, but I did not see myself as a competition sprinter in track. But like I said earlier, once I realized I could run, I felt challenged to see just what I could do. Setting records in track, traveling the United States and the world, rubbing shoulders with high officials and sports heroes is a far cry from my upbringing in the tiny community of Lynwood Park. Not many gave young black men, like me, much of a chance to succeed in life because of our impoverished and challenging surroundings.

Back in Lynwood Park, Professor Robinson, and his small staff, deserves a lot of credit for the attention they paid to students, especially young men trying to achieve success. Robinson was a stickler for all-around students. As much as he worked with my classmates on the football field, he and his staff sought to give some culture along with our brawn. Some of my classmates reminded me how Wilmer Harris, Joe Fields, James Thomas, Raymond Parks, Gene Hood, and I were part of a blackfaced minstrel show. We were decked out in black pants and navy caps. Our faces were painted black and our lips exaggerated with white chalk on and around them, while singing and tap dancing to Al Jolson's "Mammy," along with patriotic songs such as "Anchors Away." It was stereotypical, but it came from Broadway, in New York City, and that was the order of the day then.

Before he died, I can't tell you how special it was for me that Professor Robinson attended one of my track meets. He along with other teachers like Mr. Brannon, Ms. Willie Mae Hutchins, and Mr. George Gholston made lasting impressions too.

"Nobody is going to give you anything to succeed in life. Whatever you do, you've got to work hard," Mr. Gholston would always say. "You should not strive to be just as good as the person doing the same thing you are doing, but twice as well," Mr. Gholston and all the teachers used to emphasize by using slightly different words and phrases. That was a mantra that we were encouraged to heed because we were in a segregated setting.

Always inside of me, I just knew I was prepared to work hard, and twice as hard as many others, to reach my goal. The fame that I sought as a youngster came without me actively seeking it. I was in the Army stationed in Okinawa, preparing to do my part to help defend my country, when I was spotted during an on-base football game and told I was needed to run track. "Run track?" I replied to the officer who asked me. That was like asking me to play soccer; I knew what it was, but I was not really sure what I was being asked to do. To the best of my recollection, I remember racing guys in the neighborhood; but to this day, many of my old classmates, like Matthew Moore, Marvin Hood, Columbus Jones were considered pretty fast too.

Moore declares to this day, even though we are in our seventies: "Melvin was fast at 40 and 60 yards, but I could probably outrun him in the 100-yard dash."

Matthew, who had to drive to school because there was no bus for his community, is probably having a flashback to when he ran for three touchdowns to only one for me during a high school game years ago in Toccoa. Well, that is a big joke because I held the world record in the 100. Looking at my scoreboard: sixth place in the world in the 100-meter-dash with a time under ten seconds, in both the 1964 and 1968 Olympics, not to mention running the 40-yard dash in 4.0 seconds. I'm not bragging—just good.

Along with our old friends, we have often reminded Matthew that I broke sprinter Bob Hayes's record in the 70-yard dash at 6.8 seconds and tied his record in the 60-yard dash of 5.9 seconds. We also reminded him that I was part of the 1968 Olympics team of Charles Greene, Ronnie Ray Smith, and Jim Hines. We won a gold medal in the 4 x 100-meter relay in 1968 and set a world record of 38.19 seconds in the event. I was twenty-seven during the 1964 Olympics and thirty-one during the record-setting run in the 1968 Olympics. For those who are not familiar with track, most competitors are leaving track by the time they are twenty-six. At the age of thirty-five, I managed to set the world indoor record for the 50- and 70-yard dash as an amateur and 60-yard dash as a professional sprinter in 1973.

The Little Red School House

This little red school house was in our community when I came to live in Lynwood Park from Dalton. It was so different than what we were accustomed to. In Dalton we had central heating and air conditioning and the school was by no means impoverished. I was in shock to say the least, but within a year of moving there a cinder block building that wasn't much better, was built to accommodate the older children. This building had 9 rooms and no central heating. Instead, each room had a potbellied stove and its pipe ran out the window pane. What was even worse was that there was no indoor plumbing. We were provided water coolers instead for drinking water and an outhouse. The yard was red clay; Dalton's school yard was grass.

Ok, this wasn't fair I thought to myself. Why did these schools have to be so different? All schools should be the same, regardless of who attends or their economic background. I am still passionate about schools today as this experience shaped my consciousness about equality. Children are there to learn and should not be given less because of race, creed, color or economics. Schools today in this area are much better built and host many different ethnic groups. This experience pushed all of us towards integration and that was good.

Hidden Talents

> *I was surprised Mel had talent in the area of track when he went into service because we didn't have that program at our high school of Lynwood Park. We had a football team, but we probably didn't have but four scripted plays, and the rest we did off the seat of our pants. Our school's football team squad was small. We did not have enough backup players. Some of the players came to school during the football season only, and then dropped out. Our conditioning amounted of about thirty laps and fifty push-ups*
>
> *The army that Mel loved so much didn't seem to care much about him. Once a race was over, they routed him back into combat as if they didn't care whether he would survive and run, or not. We went our separate ways in joining the military. I went to the air force. We didn't meet again until Mel was in England and I was stationed in Germany.*
>
> *Mel is the most celebrated person to come out of Lynwood Park* (Robert "Sonny" Jackson, now deceased, retired bus driver for the Metropolitan Atlanta Rapid Transit Authority).

The Awakening

For as much as I enjoyed growing up in Lynwood Park, there were times I was too depressed by some things to remain impressed by other good things in the community. Lynwood Park had its share of bullies and roughnecks long before the nation realized there was such a problem. Public fights were not the rule, but they happened, sometimes in front of us and elsewhere, whether children were around to see them or not. When you are in a tiny community and you see or know about people getting killed in a location you have to pass almost every day, that does not go away quickly or easily. Most residents remember two brothers-in-law got into a fight after loud arguing on the corner at House Road and Osborne Road, and one was killed. Then there was another fight I remember when one man everyone said wouldn't harm a flea killed a neighborhood bully by using his knife to ward off an attack. He cut the man across his stomach so deeply from side to side, that the bully died as a result of the wound.

Good middle-class jobs in the community were those connected with being brick masons, carpenters, cabbies, and yardmen in the community. Much of the patio and yard work in adjoining predominantly white communities along Mabry Road, Peachtree Dunwoody Road, and Johnson Ferry Road, all adjoining my old community, bear the construction skills fostered by people like Luke Holsey, Peter Scott Sr., and Woodrow Jones. Like the cabbies, men like Mr. Willie Ed Stone worked at a county hospital; women like Mrs. Elizabeth Matthews, Mrs. Pat Martin, and Mrs. Carrie Mae Julian were nurses. Many others engaged in domestic work. For many, aspirations were dimmed by the absence of work. Military service often was the ticket to a way out.

What many in the community had that kept them going, to the detriment of many, were "love bones," or extramarital affairs. This is a term used by some for men and women they were seeing outside of their marriages. These connections resulted in kinships that were not realized until many children became teenagers or adults. There were some big public brawls that had the community talking for days. These all weighed heavily on my heart as a young boy. Why did people have to fight? Why did they have to hurt each other?

The idleness I saw could explain some of the behavior that happened; the fights and the encounters with police were usually at the community's corner spot at Osborne Road and House Road now known as Windsor Parkway. I have not been a firsthand witness to all of the killings, fighting, or bullying, but I am aware of many of them. One man, known only to me as Benny, apparently was a real bad guy. He was known to have ripped a toilet seat from the floor of his bathroom, effortlessly, and police never bothered him, regardless of any complaints involving him.

None of what I saw from police justified what I saw them doing to many black men in my neighborhood. In some cases there was police brutality, but back then no one challenged men with badges. The policeman bearing the brunt of the animosity was the one the community called Cigar. Older people say the adage of "Bad news travels fast, and good news travels slow," helps to exaggerate the negative images in my community. These actions, I think, led to many young men, adopting a strong antipolice attitude. The result was, young men from my old neighborhood were written off, and not much was expected of them but trouble. That's the firm impression I got from some members of the DeKalb County police force back then. I once told my grandmother that I wished I could find a way to get back at the police officers who seemed to randomly launch attacks on young black men, especially when they found themselves on the street corner that crisscrossed the entrance into my community, which is now called Brookhaven. I was anxious to get out of that setting.

My mind was so determined not to get caught up in what seemed to be a kind of malaise that could entrap anyone too weak to resist it. A bunch of us guys got together and formed a club called the Cavaliers. "We were not a gang, we didn't threaten or harass anyone," emphasized my buddy, Robert "Sonny" Jackson. "We didn't have a charter or anything like that, but we decided to wear black jackets and the membership was small—myself, Mel, Theodore Allen, Ralph Daniel, and William Dix," he added. "We all were pretty close. We were four guys that liked to be around each other. We saw ourselves as the good guys," Sonny Jackson said of our time together.

If a comparison were to be made, perhaps a good description of our group would be that we were cool guys who were living life in hopes of staying out of trouble and catching the eye of some of the young ladies in the community.

Cars, Cars, Cars...

Well, as you guessed it, cars have been a passion of mine, too. My first was a 1940 dark-green Ford Coupe that I bought in 1955, from money I saved while I was a caddy plus from digging foundations and working at two gas stations. All of which I did between my fifteenth and sixteenth birthday. I will never forget the day when I went down to the dealership with my grandfather, who was there to sign for the car. He trusted me and knew that I would take care of it. I had seen the car on the lot a week before and was hoping that it would still be there. To my delight, it was and I laid down $1,000 on the salesman's desk. It was money from my piggy bank and what I had tucked under my mattress. What a day that was and the proud feeling of becoming a man. I loved that car so much that you would find me always rubbing, waxing, and shining every inch of it with simonized wax. My favorite line was that "I would catch the raindrops before they landed on my car." Now I had joined the big leagues just as I remembered my dad washing his car. I even bought mud flaps for his car and the little knob you drove with. I was ten years old then and what an impression his car made on me.

I had a total of twelve cars from 1955 to 1976 when I retired from the military. They served as my means of transportation and also entertainment as I raced some of my cars at both the Fairburn Speedway and the Yellow River Speedway. My cars were of every kind and color, from a cameo 1955 Chevrolet convertible with a white top to a 1972 Jaguar sports coup and even a 1976 two-tone green Cadillac Eldorado (big car), all while I was on active duty in the military.

Today I enjoy my truck. I never thought I would buy a truck, but my wife convinced me that I should get this pretty Ford F-150 Harley Davidson truck. I love to drive it, and now feel like I'm the king on the road. It is funny how your desires change as you grow older. My need for speed isn't what it used to be, and I am grateful for the many cars that God has blessed me with.

Chapter 4

Puberty, My Manhood Reach

Lynwood Park had many pretty girls, but there was only one girl for me. We met at the beginning of seventh grade. I was fourteen, and it was love for the both of us. During our high school years, I was a star football player, and she was beautiful and popular. She was picked as the high school queen and I was the high school king. We were a pair and we were inseparable.

My high school sweetheart lived about a mile from my house with her family. Her father was a hardworking man that worked at General Motors and took care of her mother, four sisters, and one brother. We saw each other as often as we could. In the beginning, we had to sneak around, because I was scared of her daddy, mostly because I knew he was really strict on his daughters. Over time, I got to understand that I didn't have a father's hand to guide me and I surely didn't know what the outcome of my actions would bring. In those days, if a girl became pregnant, and both she and the boy were in the same school, they would have to quit school. Since I was such a good student, captain of the football team, high school king, and she as the queen, Principal Robinson made an exception and allowed me to stay. I graduated early and came back to walk with my senior class. We had about fifteen total graduates that year. I am grateful to him to this day for his support in that very difficult and defining moment in my life.

People say that when you are young, you don't know what love is. I remember the song by Nat King Cole "They Tried to Tell Us We're Too Young," but love was what I felt at the time. She was my sweetheart, only fifteen and a mother-to-be. I was not prepared to be apart from her or leave her on her own with the responsibility of our child while I moved on with my life plans. I was determined to make different choices than my father. I had to do the right thing. My mother gave her consent to a judge, and at the age of sixteen, we were married. I was on my way to being a father. Wow!

Working the Right Angles

From my earliest memories, it seems that work was a major part of my life. From selling scrap iron along with milk and drink bottles in Dalton, I had now graduated to becoming a caddy at the neighborhood country clubs, which are in the recently formed cities of Brookhaven and Dunwoody. The clubs were for whites only! What amazes me today is that these were public golf courses owned by the City of Atlanta. Blacks could not play, and I didn't think anything of it.

At Christmas, my grandparents gave me my first Schwinn bike; I was fourteen years old then. I can say that I was excited about my new bike, but not as excited as when these white guys drove through our neighborhood looking for caddies. I put aside my bike, got in their car, and nearly broke my back carrying two golf bags, but I came away rich with $10. This gave me enough money to take my little girlfriend to the movies and some to put away.

I think back to those times on my way to Capital City Country Club where no blacks could play golf, only caddy or cook. Walking the course with two golf bags on my shoulders in the hot sun to make $5 for the day, only to give a portion of it to Roy, the head caddy master, for something to eat. Roy had a side deal going with us caddies. He sold bologna sandwiches for fifty cents, moon pies for twenty-five cents, a piece of egg custard for twenty-five cents, and a drink for twenty-five cents. Now, if you were hungry you could spend a good chunk of your hard-earned money with Roy and then what most guys did, they went down the street and gambled it away on the corner. So really they went home with nothing. Not me; I was smart with my money. I'd get up early and eat something before I left my grandmother's house, like a biscuit or whatever Grandma had made. When I would make my selection with Roy, I would only spend seventy-five cents on either a bologna sandwich or egg custard and drink. Taking another $1 of my money, I'd go down to the corner to take my chance at winning, and sometimes I did and sometimes I didn't, but I always came home with at least $2 in my pocket. I found that if I saved a dollar at a time I could buy clothes for school or white bucks (shoes); I always liked to look nice and dressed to impress the girls. It felt good to have money in my pocket and to be able to spend it on things I wanted. I was really on my way to becoming a man. The golf course always gave me the worst clients because they didn't tip well, but what I got I learned to use wisely.

Fatherhood Begins

Germaine (Jobie) Pender

There were so many dreams I had about family life that I wanted to share with my very own family. Suddenly, my life had completely changed. I had graduated and survived by working any job I could get. Well, I did just that, but there was lots of manual labor. Any opportunity I got to make money I took it. I once drove a truck for a local drugstore delivering medicine. Then my father came for a visit from Chicago with my Uncle Buford. He didn't want me to stay in Georgia. He convinced me that the opportunity for work was better in Chicago and that I could go back with him for the summer.

Leaving my young pregnant wife with her parents, we piled in my dad's brand-new 1954 Chrysler. They drank all the way with me doing most of the driving. Once in Chicago, I got a job working at the Stockyard Inn Dinner Club as a dishwasher. My main job was washing silverware, and I earned enough money there to buy my new wife a diamond ring. My dad was right about making more money. That was a proud moment for me, even though it was a little diamond ring, I had big intentions.

It was hard being separated from my wife, and I missed her so much, but I stayed and worked for six months until the birth of our beautiful little girl, Germaine, whom we affectionately called Jobie. She was born July 27, 1954. When I found out that my wife was in labor, I quickly got on the next train from Chicago and reached Georgia the day after she was born. It was when our baby was about two months old that we discovered we needed more space, our own space. Up to this, point we lived with her parents. My wife's aunt had a room for rent for about $25 a week and said we could have it. Our little family now had its first little home. My friend Woodrow Jones's father gave me a job with his concrete company pushing wheelbarrows full of cement. My hands were raw from shoveling cement since I had no gloves to wear. I did this for about six months, and it was wearing on me. The harder I found myself working as a manual laborer, I found myself becoming more and more disheartened. It seemed my dreams were slipping farther and farther away from me. What I was doing was not going to give my family the life that I had always dreamed for them. This realization brought me to make one of the biggest decisions of my life. At the age of seventeen, I joined the United States Army. For many black men in my community, and elsewhere, their aspirations often have been dimmed by limited education, opportunities, or poor decision making. Military service often was a way to get focused and a means of getting an equal opportunity to get out any situation in which they found themselves. I saw a bleak future beckoning. I knew that making the decision to join the military was my opportunity to make a change for the better in our lives. It was my ticket out of my community, the South and its oppression, and a way to advance in life. I could not afford to miss this chance.

"I know of no way of judging of the future but by the past" Patrick Henry.

Chapter 5

Making the Right Move?

My first military photo age 17

"My fellow Americans, ask not what your country can do for you, ask what you can do for your country" John F. Kennedy

On March 23, 1955, I went to the recruiting office to join the United States Army. On that memorable day, there were four of us from the Lynwood Park community who said we would join up. We were required to take a test. I remember when the recruiter came to pick us up, I ended up being the only one to get into the car. No one else was to be found. We drove to the homes of each of the other three potential recruits. They could not be found. I was it. I took the test, and within two weeks, I had packed my bags and was sent to Fort Jackson, in South Carolina, for basic training. In that ride, I began to question my decision. Did I make the right move? Did my friends know something I did not?

As I began my journey on the path to a military career, it was my bus ride experience that firmed up my resolve and determination to be the best in my chosen profession. The military transport bus was full of black and white young men all going to the same place, for the same reason. It was encouraging. After all, a year earlier, the Supreme Court had handed down the *Brown vs Board of Education* decision that ended school desegregation. We were recruits headed to basic training at Fort Jackson, in South Carolina, to prepare to fight and defend our country. Well, our first stop was sixty miles east of Atlanta, in Athens, Georgia, to get something to eat. We were just across the street from the University of Georgia. When we got off the bus, the whites went in the front door and the blacks entered through the side door. I would not get off the bus to use the bathroom, I guess in protest, so needless to say I suffered the remainder of my ride to Fort Jackson. Naively perhaps, I thought that when I joined the army, despite the color of my skin, I would be treated the same as any other soldier. Again I would ask the question *why*? I thought I could do the same as whites and be given respect as a soldier, ready and willing to fight and die for this country. That bus ride did something special for me. It opened my eyes to the reality of life as a black man in this wonderful country of ours. Nothing had changed. I still had to go in the other door, use the Colored Only facilities, and sit in the back of the bus.

Let me digress for a minute. Racial hatred is a learned behavior. We were not born to hate people just because they are a different color or look different from us. We cannot, and must not, lump everyone in one race into one basket because of the actions of a few.

When I was around twelve or thirteen years old, I was a caddy at a golf course near my grandparents. I would take used clubs and burn the head off the wooden shafts, replacing the wood with tree branches, and then my friend Jimmy and I would practice in the dirt under my grandmother's car port. One day, there was a bunch of my friends on the corner hitting balls into an open field. There was a house maybe two hundred yards from where we were hitting them. We had some guys that were very talented, taking a five iron, not knowing they could hit it 150 yards where the house stood. We knew the ball flew out of the neighborhood and hit a white man's house. He came over with a vengeance accusing me and calling me the N-word. My grandmother made me shut up and get in the house. It didn't change me to hate people because of their color. I only found myself challenged by the ones that would say negative things about people to hurt them because of the color of their skin.

Notwithstanding my admiration for Audie Murphy, I was somewhat disillusioned with the United States Army which was trying to place limitations on my dreams of excellence and recognition. I was torn. On the one hand, I was so discouraged about the issue of race in America. On the other hand, however, I felt optimistic and compelled to do what I could to bring about change. This change was not only for me but for all the others that would follow me. I had a new purpose, and it gave me an even stronger drive, to be the best at what I was doing, and to be recognized as the best by everyone, both black and white.

Chapter 6

Mel: The Black Knight

"Faith is taking the first step even when you don't see the whole staircase" Martin Luther King Jr.

Nowhere in my résumé of life and racing have I sought to rescue a damsel in distress. I am not a person of high birth. However, I have tried to let my light shine, and the beams from it have touched some throughout this nation, and other parts of the world, and they have shared their views with me regarding different phases of my life. They have expressed my impact on their lives.

Army: A New Adventure

During the ages of seventeen, eighteen, and nineteen, these days, responsibility and discipline are two phases of life that often are eased into children in their late teens. I did not have that luxury. Key phases of my young adult life were thrust upon me, mostly because I had no other options. In many ways, I had to become a man by myself based largely on what my mother and grandfather taught me.

Once at Fort Jackson, my assignment was in the 101st Airborne Basic Training Battalion. I worked hard to prove myself and mastered all my tests, achieving the number one position in the physical training test results. Getting a weekend pass was unheard of for someone in basic training, but I got one. As a result of my performance, I was given a pass to go see my wife and baby.

Serving in the army was a new experience, a growing-up experience, but military officials did not know that like them, I was on a mission. I was determined to keep my vow to work hard and do whatever it took to be the best I could be at whatever they threw my way. For me, being the best was just that. I was on a journey that would mark over twenty years of military service until I retired in 1976.

I tried to keep my surroundings neat and in order. I kept my uniform up to snuff, and those who served with me will agree that PFC (private first class) Pender was the sharpest-looking guy in the company. They could see how seriously I took my appearance, especially on guard duty. My clothes and shoes were impeccable, my locker and bed were the best kept and cleanest. In my plan, I had to do something to be recognized if I was going to get anywhere at all. To my surprise, and dismay, I would soon learn that for the most part, black soldiers were treated no differently in the military than when they were civilians. If you wanted to achieve something other than truck driving, cooking, or serving as a construction engineer and all other hard labor jobs, you had to push yourself toward a higher standard of excellence than that expected of white colleagues. One absolutely had to go the extra mile. This was reinforced beyond any doubt on my second eight weeks of training at Fort Leonard Wood, Missouri. I was not at all happy when they assigned me as a construction worker. I had sufficient experience doing laborious jobs to know it was not what I wanted to spend my life doing. My determination was to find a way out of this type of assignment. The *Brown vs Board Education* decision that outlawed school segregation had given me, and other African American people, reason to be optimistic, and the expected equality many of us saw in the military was a good way to get there.

Chapter 7

Operation Skywarf

After basic training in 1955, I was shipped out on a naval vessel called the USS *Patch* headed to England. It took us seven days to get there, and I was sick as a dog all the way. My duties required very little skill—peeling potatoes, cleaning toilets, and scrubbing the decks. Since I was afflicted with severe seasickness, these duties only lasted two days. It was my first boat ride, and it convinced me that I could never be a sailor in the Navy. Our operation was called Operation Skywarf. We were sent there to rebuild airstrips for the British Air Force that had been destroyed by the Germans. The military at that time was still helping to rebuild Europe following WWII. Stanstead Airport, now used as a civilian airport, was to be my home for the next eighteen months. When we got off the ship and I saw my living quarters, it was clear that we were in for a rough time. Our housing was called Quonset huts. These were semiround buildings made out of tin with two potbelly stoves positioned at each end of the quarters for heat.

In England the weather was a combination of rain, fog, and cold most of the time. Coming from the warmth of Georgia, this was much to which I had to get accustomed. My assignment was to be a carpenter, and they put me to work wherever they needed me.

We worked long, hard hours in cold rain since we were on a tight schedule to have the airstrip completed. In my determination to find a better way forward, I made myself "shine" during my guard duty. I knew from my previous experience that this was one area that I could attract attention by standing out from the other soldiers. My boots where spit-shined so well that you could see yourself on them. As for my uniform, it always had razor-sharp creases. My weapon was squeaky clean, and I was polished. My actions resulted in my promotion to driving the construction foreman's three-quarter-ton truck. No more walking for me, and I also had days off.

In England

My Quonset hut quarters

I took pride in my new assignment and kept the three-quarter-ton truck spotless. I would put sandbags to act as makeshift floor mats for the foreman's feet. It was sharp. My next promotion came and led to me driving the company commander's jeep. He rarely went anywhere, but I was moving up. A milestone came for me after about six months; I was promoted to driving the battalion commander's sedan. Wow! I had become the number one chauffeur in Operation Skywarf. For me, this was a great improvement from driving big trucks, digging ditches, or working in cement plants. I was clean every day and had spare time to play basketball, and I even took up golf. All these took place between the ages of seventeen and nineteen.

Once in England, I would not go out anywhere or do anything else but work. I was devoted to my wife and did not want to go to the clubs looking for women like the older other guys in my unit. Instead, I took up a profitable sideline in sales and public relations.

In the parlance of the street, I became a hustler, selling cigarettes and gin to the local pubs. And like my father demonstrated early in life, it proved profitable.

I was not doing anything illegal, just doing what men do to make ends meet. I made enough extra money to have some suits made for myself and send extra money home to my family. It was at a pub in Bishop Stafford that I learned how to throw darts. It was a pastime that I grew to love. On my eighteenth birthday, I was taken out to the USO (an officers') Club in London called the Marlowe House. It was there that I experienced my first mixed drink called a Singapore Sling. I noticed that people in London dressed in sharp suits and cashmere coats. I wanted to look just as good as they did too. My new suits purchased from my sideline business ensured that I did. As an eighteen-year-old, I could legally go out on my own. London became my regular haunt. I experienced jazz music at Piccadilly Circle. I loved it, and every chance I got, I would take the train from Bishop Stafford to London to get my fill of jazz music. However, it seemed that we always missed the last train going back to base. Since we had to get back somehow, the only way was to catch what was called the Milk Train, a late-night freight train. We had to hop the train, fancy clothes and all.

England was a great experience. Not only did I progress in the army, I also learned how to survive and use the military system to improve my lifestyle. I put some of my grandfather's advice to work for me to "be the best you can be and be the best in life." This applied even when working as a construction worker in England, even though I did not really enjoy it. Throughout my life, I have found it important that I perform at the best of my abilities in whatever assignment, position, or circumstance. I have seen that excellence, more than likely, has led to promotions than mediocrity, self-pity, or complacency. Everyone must learn to make the best of every situation in which they find themselves. The promotions, rewards, and blessings come when you least expect them. This was true for me, and my key was to keep "shining" in the places and positions where I found myself in. The same thing can work for others.

Chapter 8

From Cheerio to Howdy!

"Change is the law of life. And those who look only to the past or present are certain to miss the future"

John F. Kennedy

After eighteen months in England, I was reassigned to Fort Walters, Texas, where a helicopter school was being built. I was with a group of soldiers responsible for all the construction at the school. We did anything that involved construction and maintenance. Once I returned to the United States, my family joined me. This was such a great joy. We got a two-bedroom trailer in the town of Mineral Wells, Texas, where my wife and daughter spent most of their time. Our landlord, a black man, was what you would call a slumlord. The trailer was old and "raggedy," but it was clean. In the meantime, we made a request to live in the house he owned in the back and were waiting for it to become vacant. The time came for us to move in. The landlord sprayed for roaches that day. We proceeded to move our stuff in, and that night, we had the fright of our lives. There were wall-to-wall roaches. They descended on our living quarters like a well-trained miniature army on maneuvers. When we saw this we all ran out screaming. The next morning, we moved back to our ragged trailer until another trailer became available on base, and where we stayed for the duration of my posting at Fort Walters.

At the end of a one-year assignment, I reenlisted in the 82nd Airborne Division and I was sent to Fort Bragg, North Carolina. Could it be, I asked myself? Am I on the road to realizing a dream of being a pilot and flying planes?

I knew soldiers in the airborne unit jumped out of planes, so I figured there was a way I would end up realizing one of my dreams of flying one. Still, I was on top of the world because I realized I would be jumping out of an airplane and flying, just not the way I envisioned. My love for what I was doing resulted in nine years of service with the 82nd Airborne Division.

My recreation outlet was playing football, and we had a great team. It was about eight months after being at Fort Bragg that I suffered my first major injury while playing football. I often played both offense and defense. I went to tackle a guy, and his knee came up and hit me square in my jaw. The next thing I knew I was waking up in the hospital with a neck collar. Being knocked unconscious, I cannot tell you anything about how I got to the hospital. What I do know is that I suffered a concussion and fractured vertebrae. The doctor said I would never jump out of planes again. That it would be too dangerous.

Never say never to me!

There was a fire inside me that could not be quenched, a desire that would not succumb to opposition, even if it was my own body that screamed enough.

"Just watch me!" was my silent response to the doctor's prognosis.

Any athlete worth his salt will tell you that unless there is an illness that is life-threatening, the likelihood of stopping an athlete from engaging in something he sees as enjoyable, fun, challenging, competitive, or necessary is very unlikely. It was about three months into my healing process when I had an urgent need for some extra cash. The army paid us $55 dollars a month to jump, and I had not jumped in three months. Remember, I had a family, and I needed the money. A friend of mine, Rex Harris, often grabbed an extra parachute and made a jump with me out of helicopters.

My financial difficulty was just the extra push I needed. All it took to qualify for the $55 was one jump. So naturally, I went against the doctor's orders and did the jump. I continued jumping regularly, like everyone else. In fact, during my time of being airborne, I did seventy-nine jumps. Some were in America and others were in the Philippines, Korea, Alaska, and Okinawa.

One of our field exercises was to land on a particular mountain in the Philippines. When we landed, we encountered a group of mountain people called "Mountain Yards". They were small and lived inside the mountain. They barely had on clothes and lived in little shacks about the size of a twelve-by-twelve room, and there were as many as twelve people in one house. We found all kinds of Japanese artifacts left behind from World War II.

When we jumped over Korea, it was over the Hahn River. By now, I was the captain in charge and called out "Red light!" to signal it was time to jump.

As pleasant as the weather was in some locations where we jumped, Alaska was brutal. It was so cold there that whatever we wore was inadequate. We had boots we called Mickey Mouse boots strapped to the skis we had to wear, but they wouldn't stay on. I strained my back lugging the super heavy backpacks we used to carry our supplies. It seemed to hurt more because of the cold. Despite the cold, the nights in Alaska were extremely beautiful. A display of colored lights blazed across the sky each night called the Northern Lights. It was a light show greater than anything I had ever seen.

Old people had an adage they would tell disobedient younger ones: "A hard head makes for a soft back." The cumulative effect of these jumps was very demanding on my body, and I paid a price in health because of those jumps. Today I pay for my ambitions with the adverse health effects that have materialized—but I would not change a single one of those jumps. Nope.

My first paratrooper photo

One of my jumps

Chapter 9

Homeland Disrespect: Still a Reason to Hope

By now, the army had become racially integrated, and with it came many readjustments. When I first joined the army, I was placed in an all-black troop, and even though we didn't get the same jobs as the white enlisted men, we understood each other. Now that segregation was no longer legal, many changes were being implemented. There had always been racial tension, but not to the extent that we experienced in civilian life. However, as a part of integration, I became a member of a racially mixed troop of American soldiers. I had witnessed real change in my lifetime. Equality for all people, soldiers and civilians alike, was becoming a greater reality. That does not mean that tensions did not persist. One seemingly small but significant incident comes to mind that took place at around this time. It was prior to my leaving for Okinawa. We had been delayed for five days. All the men in my unit had been given leave until it was time to for us to ship out. My intent was to go to Atlanta and visit with my family. Since my time was short and taking the bus would be long, a few of the white soldiers suggested we hitchhike our way back. I had never hitched a ride before, so I was relying on the other guys. When we got out on the highway they huddled together for a chat. The next thing I knew, one soldier said, "We'll see you later!"

The soldiers walked off down the road, leaving me behind. I guess they felt that they would not get picked up being with a black person. Well, I wasn't sure what to do next. It was pitch-dark out, raining, and frankly I was scared. Eventually, a black guy came along, gave me a ride to a small town nearby, dropping me off at the service station. I thought I might be able to catch a bus from there. Well, I sat down to wait, and to my surprise, a car pulled up full of white guys: "You need a ride?" the driver yelled out.

"I am going to Atlanta," I told him.

"Hop in!" he said, and they took me all the way to Peachtree Street in downtown Atlanta. Now these guys also were in the military, and they did not know me, yet they were kind enough to look out for me. But the same guys I had spent almost every day with, that I would have to fight side by side with, face life-and-death situations with, deserted me as soon as civilian streets beckoned. What happened was ironic, but at the same time, the end result of the incident was inspiring. There is always reason to hope, to believe that change for the better is possible. You see, I believe that as long as there are some good people in this world, then good, decent principles will win out over the bad ones, even if it takes time. Patience is a virtue, and hope for progress in human relations is a necessary first ingredient for anyone who dreams of a better future in a better society.

Chapter 10

Relationships

It had now come to the place where my military career had become a detriment to my marriage. In short, we were having differences that were heightened by my determinations to fulfill the dreams I had, that I thought we both shared. For men with a dedication like mine to the military, it was like having a mistress. Being in the military is a hardship on both the husband and wife, and both people need to have a clear understanding that a military career involves a lot of personal sacrifices. When you are in the military, it owns you. When you are told to go on an assignment, you are given orders to go. In short, when they say jump, your response is not what, but how high. I was fully committed to my military career, and I was also dedicated to my family. My first obligation was to my family, but there were demands associated with a military career, especially in my case that I know neither my first wife nor the two after her could have imagined.

At one point during my career, I wanted to get a college education, and that meant I had to spend more time away from my family. Later during another marriage, I spent time away training and competing. When all the commitments I had were added up, they proved to be disastrous in terms of what I wanted to do with my family.

Military demands for me were exacerbated by the fact that I was involved in military athletics, and I was being groomed for the Olympics. I can understand how my first wife, and two others with whom I tried to share love, could feel a certain amount of insecurity, betrayal, and abandonment that simply could not be resolved.

I got married young because I wanted to have a family. The opportunities began to come in the form of scholarship offers to college. I believe in family and always will. The effects on me of my parents' divorce caused me to make a commitment to myself that I would not put my child through those same painful experiences and that I would do my best to make my marriage work. I know I wanted my father to stay with me and for us to be a family. In my own situation with my first wife, we were young and there were many ups and downs in our relationship. Later on in my career, I concluded that the forming of a marital union was nearly impossible until my career as a competitor ended. For me, making a commitment to success drew me farther away from any time that could be given to the family. My movement toward success would eventually leave my first wife behind, and after eighteen years, we would come to end our relationship.

Marriage is an investment, and if your life is too busy with other things, you really can't make that investment. After two other marriages, I found my soul mate in my fourth and final wife, Pastor Debbie Pender. The family I had envisioned as the two of us is now a blended one with six children, nine grandchildren, and one great-grandchild. Debbie's and my connection came unexpectedly. I wasn't looking, and she wasn't either. We met in a church parking lot. Debbie is a minister, and she had just come back to the States from England, after living there for three years. She had been invited to my church and was talking with my pastor outside after the service. We shook hands, and neither one of us wanted to let go. I knew then that we had something special. I had told myself that I would never marry again, but now I know that God sent her to me. After many dates, and several marriages, I have found my soul mate. You don't know what true happiness is until it comes. You may chase after it, and desire it, but it is truly a gift and one to be cherished.

Chapter 11

Fame Found Me on Foreign Soil

Winning my first race

First race victory stand 1961

My next military posting was overseas in 1960. This time I was on Japanese soil. Okinawa an island off Japan has about three hundred thousand people and is approximately twenty-five miles long. It was a completely different world to any previous experience I had gone through. The people were hardworking, intelligent, and very polite. This was the first time a group of people had shown me so much respect. It was new to me, and I loved it. For the first time I felt free as I interacted with them. The shackles of stereotypes and expectations of prejudice melted away, and I felt really good about myself. I quickly realized that the absence of racial barriers with these people was the reason for my feeling of well-being, acceptance, and almost-happy self-abandonment. However, once I was back among the soldiers, the legacy of segregation, discrimination, and poor expectations was still there. It was such a shame to be on foreign soil, to be from the same country, yet still be fighting among ourselves, treating each other unkindly, unfairly, and unequally. Why? Why did this have to be?

My rank at the time was sergeant or "buck" sergeant Pender. I wore three stripes, and I was a squad leader for ten men that I had to guide and train for combat. I had to make sure the men learned different tactics in order to serve in real combat situations. I continued in my love of football and was on the Army Ranger football team. I had still retained my position as a halfback.

Military higher-ups sent out a request for fast runners to participate in the base's Friendship Track Meet. The track meet was an event the islanders used to build friendly relations between the people on the island and the military troops stationed there. Since I was his fastest man on the team, the coach told me, "I want you to go to the gym supply room, see the supply clerk, pick up some track shoes, some shorts, and a top. Someone will pick you up in the morning and take you to Nago"—which is the northernmost part of the island—"to run against the Japanese Olympic team from Osaka, Japan, who were training for the 1964 Olympics, and the Okinawans."

"Coach, what are you talking about? Run Track?" I asked. I never ran track in my life! I wouldn't know the first thing to do?" I continued.

"Just follow the other guys and do what they do," my coach replied with a laugh. "They won't beat you anyway," he added. I said okay and that was that.

I went to the supply room to pick up the equipment my coach had told me to get. The shoes scared me. They looked to me as if they had come from outer space. They were black leather shoes with permanent spikes at least two inches long and the shoe tongue had to be longer than the shoestrings. Ugly, ugly, ugly, that's all I can say. But this was my first time ever seeing a pair of track shoes. I did not know what they were supposed to look like. I can admit now that I was preoccupied with looking sharp and wishing they had made better-looking shoes. Participation in the event turned out to be my defining moment.

A Great Change

I was totally unprepared for the turn that my life took next. As it turned out, an enduring change was about to impact my life in a most pleasant and satisfying manner. I was picked up by a jeep the next morning and driven to Nago. When I arrived, I went into shock. There had to be at least a thousand people there. I thought it was going to be a very small, friendly event. When I saw all those people, my heart started pounding in my chest, and I said to myself, "What have I gotten myself into?" Remembering what the coach had told me, I wandered around and did exactly what he said. I watched the other runners. I watched them as they warmed up and went through their routine, getting ready for the race. I acted confidently, conveying the image of someone who knew what it was about, and I did exactly what all the other runners present were doing. I often wondered if they guessed that I was a novice. I didn't have starting blocks so when the others got down into those things they called starting blocks, I dug two holes in the ground and tucked my feet in. When the gun went off, they started running. I said to myself, "I guess I better run." They were leading most of the way down the track, but I caught up to them, and the crowd went crazy with excitement. I won the race, and after hearing the crowd making lots of noise, I knew I must have done something impressive. Well, I did not know what all the fuss was about. I just ran as fast as I had done many times before. I was twenty-five years old and I had just discovered another dimension to myself, another aspect of my natural abilities that would give rise to more dreams to succeed in life, be somebody, and gain recognition. The experience also reminded me that if one listens and obeys, you never know what awaits you around the next corner. Arriving back at the base, I immediately went to the football coach's office and told him of my experience.

"I knew it. You are the fastest little guy I've ever seen," my coach said.

He then told me that when the track team season came around, he would like to see me compete. I listened, and I did. I was undefeated in the 100-yard and 200-yard dash, winning the Inner Service

Championship and becoming the Pacific Champion. As a result of my track victories, I was awarded seven days of leave in Yokohama, Japan. That is on the mainland. We had a great time. That is when I discovered that the people on the mainland were even nicer. There were so many people on bicycles, there were taxis they called rickshaws where they used people like horses, pulling other people in a chair. There were bright lights, and the great smell of the Japanese food enticed me to partake of their culinary delights. What a beautiful and delightful place. The last day of our leave was the most special. I was with the guys at the NCO Club and one of my teammates was escorting two beautiful Japanese ladies. The name of one lady I met was Monaco Yokamoto. She was intriguing, and I was enthralled by her beauty and mannerisms. She mentioned to me that the 1964 Olympic Games would be in Tokyo. I told her, "I will be back and I will be on that team, just so I can see you again." She smiled and said, "We will see." Well, I did not know much about the Olympics or the track team, and I had no idea how to even go about getting onto the team. I just knew that I wanted to come back to Japan, one way or the other. Overseas was great because we were not black or white, just Americans.

The Army Track Team

I was still stationed in Okinawa when several colleges read about me running in the Army Times Newspaper. My exceptional times posted when I ran in Okinawa, and the Inner Service Championship made me a prime candidate for recruiting by track coaches of major colleges around United States. Excited at the prospect of receiving a college education, I got out of the military in 1962 and went back to Georgia to pursue my dream. I was given a track college scholarship to go to Clark College of Atlanta (now Clark Atlanta University), but I decided not to take it.

Once again, the need to support my family was a major deciding factor. Marital discord once again reared its ugly head as I had to make a decision that would force me to make a decision.

Before the year was finished, I reenlisted and was sent to the 101st Airborne Division at Fort Campbell, Kentucky. After six months I was given orders for Korea. It was in Korea that I learned more about the army track team. It was my friend Richard Whitfield who came to me one day and said that he knew a way that I could run for the army. Richard had been our center on the football team, and he knew my speed. He had read about the army looking for track and field athletes to join the team. While still in Korea, we wrote a letter and requested that I join the track team when I returned to the United States. Well, I was accepted and reassigned to the 82nd Airborne Division, Charlie Company 325. They put me to work in the Army Supply at Fort Bragg, North Carolina. The army's sports branch granted me two hours a day for training, which was to get me ready to join the track team in Fort Hood, Texas. There was much controversy among my superiors about me being an athlete and having training time allocated to me. It seemed to me that the sergeant where I worked did not like jocks. One day when I came to work I found out I had been transferred to another company with the 82nd Airborne Division. I could not believe what had just happened to me. Here I was with permission from the US Sports Department in Washington DC, to train and yet that did not seem to matter to my superiors

I was not prepared to give up on my training or the chance of winning more medals. What I had to do was clear. I had to report this mistreatment. Calling the sports branch, I informed them of what was happening. Their intervention seemed to make matters worse though because I was then assigned to a special service department. I was the only black man in that department, and the jobs they gave me made me feel underappreciated, undervalued, and overworked. I painted fences, raked lawns, and did every manual chore that would keep me out of the office. They stationed me down on the football field in a little shack. Out of sight, and alone, I had a private battle of disappointment, embitterment, and even despair. I was in the middle of an overtly discriminatory and unjust situation designed to keep me down. Now, my inner strength, my spirit began to fight for my destiny. I viewed myself as a special child of the Most High God. He had given me a talent, and that was my way out of this mess.

Chapter 12

Practice, Practice, Practice

Arise and shine for your light has come and the glory of the Lord is upon you.

—Isaiah 60:1

I knew that it was not my time to pass out of the light and into the darkness of oblivion. Training with all my might and determination, fueling all my frustration into my efforts would prove a wise tactic. In 1963, I had only one year to train and be good enough to succeed at the Inner Service Championships, get through the tryouts for the 1964 Olympic Games, and qualify to be in Japan. Just at the right time, I was transferred to Fort Hood, Texas, and made the track team. I was assigned a real coach, Cornell Lipscomb. He was affectionately known as the Whip, and he was as tough as nails.

Lipscomb demanded respect, 110 percent commitment, and total involvement in the training schedule. He pushed me so hard that at times I thought I would die. I ran so hard I suffered shin splints. My teammates would laugh at me because I would cut off the sleeves of my sweatshirts to make bandages. I would wrap my legs up every night plastered in analgesics. Coach didn't care how much I hurt; he ran me even harder. He knew very well what I was up against and what it took to succeed in the Olympics. He held the secret to making a champion out of me, and once again, I must listen and obey. One thing I can say is thank God for Coach Lipscomb. He shaped and molded me into the sprinter that I finally became. God gives us talents, but it is up to us to develop them. A talent is just a seed full of potential and possibilities; but hard work, patience, perseverance and faith can transform it into a great treasure.

I continued to practice hard that year. I ran in every meet I could, winning numerous indoor and outdoor championships in the 100-meter and 100-yard dash. It was at the 1963 Amateur Athletic Union Championship in St. Louis, Missouri, that I met sprinter Bob Hayes for the first time, along with other top runners in America.

Chapter 13

Qualifying for the 1964 Olympics

"For a righteous man falls seven times, and rises again, but the wicked stumble in time of calamity" (Proverbs 24:16 NASB)

I was truly scared. A different scared than that experienced in combat, but still scared. You know, fear can be a good thing sometimes. It tells you when to stop and when to run. In this instance, it propelled me to run one of the best races of my life. I won in record time. My credibility rating hiked. I was now being ranked with some of the greats. I was on my way to establishing a place and a name for myself in the world of track and field.

It was clear to me that in order to qualify for the 1964 Olympics, I had to make the right impression at the Inner Service Championships also. The first tryouts were held at Randall's Island, New York, and then in Los Angeles, California, but I still did not have enough running experience under my belt. Running for the army in Baltimore, Maryland, I won the 100-yard dash in 9.5 seconds. This made a great impression on the track coach for the Philadelphia Pioneer

Track Club. He asked me to join them. This was an opportunity to gain more experience, and I took it. I traveled with the club all over the United States and Canada. It was during this time that I came face-to-face, again, with continuing racism—a curse that threatened to undermine the personal growth and progress I had achieved. My friend Chappell and I were in our army uniforms stationed in the 82nd Airborne Division at Fort Bragg, North Carolina. We were getting ready to leave Baltimore and return to our post. On our way to the bus station, we stopped at a diner nearby to get some food. As soon as we opened the door, a waitress blocked our path. She told Chappell that I could not enter. He could, she said, he was white, but since I was black, they did not accept "my kind" in their diner. Chappell was outraged and gave her a piece of his mind. How dare she deny his friend the right to be treated as any other soldier representing our country, he made his demand through clenched teeth, trying to restrain himself.

I reflected on the progress that "my kind" had achieved since I first joined up as a hopeful recruit in Atlanta, Georgia, back in 1955. The changes that the army had implemented by integrating may have brought much needed improvements, but the rest of America was still way behind. This was another one of my *why* moments. We so badly needed to come together as a country if we were to realize our place in the destiny of mankind and our role in the world as leaders and defenders of freedom. The incident was merely to remind me to strive harder, be smarter, aim higher, and work patiently to overcome the many barriers of racism in all its guises. I want my children and grandchildren to inherit a just and more equitable society. I had grown since leaving Lynwood Park, and my experiences spurred me on to succeed in every situation that I encountered.

The Inner Service Championships was held in Quantico, Virginia, on the Quantico Marine Base. I was a winner there and went on to the tryouts in California. I placed among the top three athletes. I was picked along with Bob Hayes and Trent Jackson to run the 100-meter race in Japan as a member of the United States Olympics Track and Field Team.

Let me jump ahead, since I am reflecting on injustice, to what awaited me after the 1964 Olympics Games. I was given a week's leave to go home, and upon coming back to the base at Fort Bragg, North Carolina, I arrived to nothing. There was a total disregard for my involvement in the Olympics. I had expected at least a "Congratulations, Mel" from my superiors. Instead, I was greeted with a harsh "Where have you been?" I had imagined that I would at least have been complimented on my achievement. There was nothing. I was treated as if I had committed some kind of offense. I was injured and still performed among the best runners in the world.

At the 1964 Olympics, the welcome by the Japanese was overwhelming. My soul was stirred by the colorful sights and sounds. Behind all the pomp and circumstance, though, were the pigeons and doves. What about the birds you ask? Well, it is a tradition to set pigeons or doves free when we take the opening ceremony lap. That's when everyone ducks for cover because of the flying poop. Those who had been involved in other Olympics before knew to bring newspapers with them, but those of us who didn't will never forget that moment.

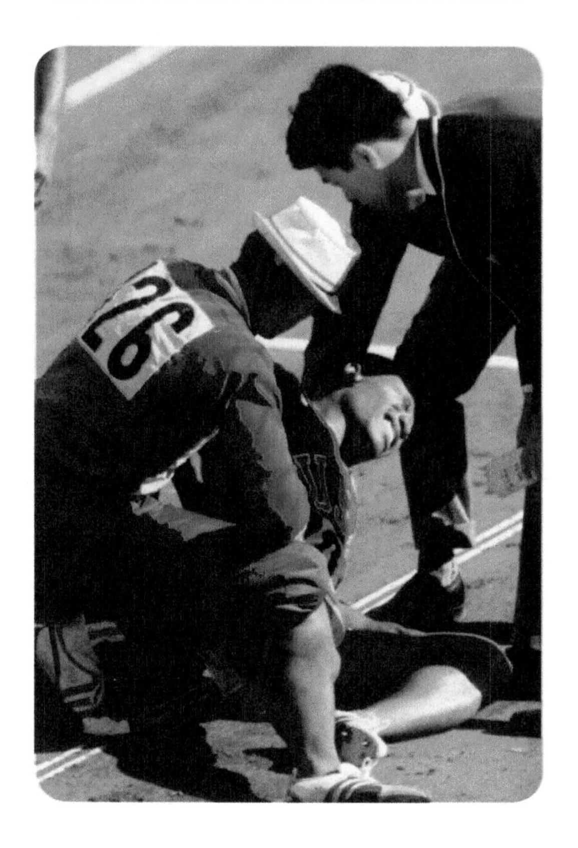

1964 Olympics injury

The opening ceremony was huge and spectacular. Lyndon Baines Johnson, of Texas, was president then, and our team wore white cowboy hats and dressed like Texans to represent him.

After much hype and good times, my hopes were dashed in my first Olympics when I finished sixth in what I thought was going to be my best event. I had injured myself horsing around with my teammate Trenton Jackson a couple of days before the event. Unbeknown to me, this caused me to have torn muscles around my rib casing. The doctor gave me injections, taped me up, and told me not to run, but I ran nonetheless and pulled up lame in the quarterfinals. Trenton pulled a muscle as well in his quarterfinals and was unable to compete. I continued to run in the finals, and because of my injury, I was replaced by Paul Drayton in the 4 x 100 meter relay. Trenton was also replaced by Gerald Ashworth. Still, I recorded the sixth best time in the world and at the age of twenty-seven. Sprinters normally stop running before that age.

I was glad Paul Drayton was my replacement. In life, you meet people that have a powerful impact on your life, and Paul was one of those people. He was a true Christian. He was smart and could quote the Bible word for word and live it. We were roommates while traveling across the country and Europe. I was neat, and he was messy. We would often laugh about our differences. Once, my peculiar friend shaved the hair off his entire body and told us he didn't want anything slowing him down.

I went to the hospital because of my injury, and during my two days of recuperation, I could not help thinking what I could have done had I stayed healthy. I believe I would have won one or two gold medals, and Bob would have been watching my rear end. My stay in the hospital provided me with lots of time to think. I thought my running days were over because, at the age of twenty-seven very few continue with a future as a sprinter. A higher education was one of the things on my mind. Then I made a promise to myself to get into a college. For some time, I had been pondering the prospect of becoming an officer. Since there was no way out but up, when I returned to Fort Bragg, I took the test for Officer Candidate School (OCS) and passed with flying colors. There was a special waiver made because of my age, and I was accepted.

Chapter 14

The Making of an Officer

"The battle, sir, is not to the strong alone; it is to the vigilant, the active, the brave"

Patrick Henry

I was sent to Fort Benning, Georgia, to begin my training to become an officer.

Physically, the training was the toughest months of military life. It was in week eighteen of field training that I got sick. It was a major exercise during my officer training. We were out for three days on survival training exercises called escape and evasion. The exercise was to teach us how to escape if we got captured by the enemy. And the training meant we were actually experiencing torture techniques likely to be used by the enemy if any of us got caught during combat. Naturally, the first thing that happened was that we were "captured" and put in "prison." Then the torture began. They tied us to trees with chains. We then had to kneel on logs without slipping off. If we fell off, we were hit. They put us in holes and placed fifty-gallon drums over our heads. They then beat the drums continuously with a stick. After all that, we would be interrogated, tied to a chair, and screamed at abusively with the sole purpose of breaking down self-control, self- esteem, confidence, and composure.

While on these exercises, we got our food from the partisans. They were the civilians. They would bring us one chicken, two ducks, and a can of rice. This had to feed thirty men for three days, and we had to find a way to cook it. Additionally, in each rice can there were compasses and maps. The maps gave us directions on how to get back to the trucks once we succeeded in escaping. Now if you became ill, you had to reach a point on the road where the medics would pick you up and take you back to the sick bay. It was raining when we finally escaped. We had to cross a creek that had swollen from the rainwater. My shoelaces had rotted and my boot got stuck in the mud while crossing. I had to dive under the water, retrieve my boot, and continue the mission. I had become severely dehydrated during all the interrogations and, by the time we made it to the road, too sick to continue; I was left there. The medics picked me up and took me to the hospital where I spent a day there being fed intravenously and then was sent back to my unit. After a month, I found myself sick again and this time was out for ten days. I had to repeat six weeks of training because I had failed to complete the course. I was right back to square one, survival training. My superiors were always on me. It seems they never let up. I was convinced that it was because I was an Olympian. At age twenty-seven, I was the oldest man in the class. "Never give up," I kept telling myself. I had to obtain a special waiver to get into OCS. There were people in charge that tried to break me, break my spirit, so I would want to give up. But they had the wrong target. I did not know how to give up.

There was another incident during my quest to become an officer that I couldn't let pass. I was forced by a training officer to eat corn bread. It might not sound like much of an issue at first hearing, but I never liked corn bread during the best of times. A lieutenant, whom we had nicknamed Baby Huey after a cartoon duck, and fresh out of college ROTC, was brought in to train us to be officers. He seemed to know very little about being in the military and felt he had to do something to prove himself to his superiors. On one occasion, he chose to make an example of me. Military food is not always the best, and that day, the corn bread tasted horrible to me, so I left it on my plate. Well, the lieutenant was incensed. He ordered me to stand at attention and then stuff my mouth with the remaining corn bread. It was such a humiliating experience. I was so upset over the incident that I went straight to the commanding officer and made a formal verbal grievance. The commanding officer must have taken care of it because I saw very little of the lieutenant after that, and he never bothered me again.

It is very important that we know when to suffer in silence and when to speak up. After all, "wisdom is the better part of valor," and every black person who has had to navigate the choppy waters of discriminatory practices in order to succeed knows or learns this profound truth. Yet there are times when some things cannot be allowed to pass without comment or action. For me, this was one of those times. However, despite all the hassles that I endured, I completed OCS and was commissioned an officer in the United States Army. From a young seventeen-year-old who went into the military, as the only way to realize a desire to provide for my family and achieve a measure of success in life, I was now seeing a milestone in my career of which I could truly be proud.

"That's my boy!" beamed Grandmother Wowa during my graduation. She knew my story of struggle and let the pride she had in me explode. I didn't mind at all. It gave me joy to see her and other members of my family at the graduation ceremonies.

My experiences at OCS permanently changed the way I viewed myself. During many of my years growing up, I was told that I was not smart enough, that I would not amount to anything. Many in society viewed me, and other young black men, as uneducable and treated us as less than human beings because of the color of our skin. Yet it was in OCS that I found out that I had a high IQ above the standard in which to become an officer. It was at this pivotal point in my life that I stopped believing the lies that had been forced on me in the segregated society I had grown up in. With this newfound revelation, I realized I had the freedom to be all that I was destined to be, and no one could hold me down, or back. It is about choices. The choices you make at crucial times in your life will affect your future.

It was all up to me from here on out. At last, I had received my wings to fly, to soar, just like an eagle.

It was not long after becoming an officer, I was sent to Vietnam. My mission, along with that of Second Lieutenant Rod Morris, was to get the facilities ready for the incoming troops. We were part of an advance party that had flown to Vietnam in a special plane. As Rod recalls, the temperature in Vietnam was 100 degrees, and when we got the off the plane, we were given guns with no ammunition. This was totally insane to us, but we were fortunate not to have met any Vietcong on our arrival. We were brought to the base camp to set it up for our battalion, which was 3rd Battalion 60th Infantry. This had to be done over a two-week period, which caused us to work fast. It had to be stocked and supplied with goods for the incoming troops. Sufficient living quarters needed to be set up, which involved putting up lights, showers, dining hall benches and tables, everything that would make the troops feel comfortable. It was done in record time and Lieutenant Colonel Chamberlain was so impressed and made it a point to thank us. I guess being task-oriented is why employers seem to like *commissioned and noncommissioned military personnel* working for them, because we often are task-oriented and used to getting things done right, and on time.

Courageous, Confident, Capable

"Many people don't realize Mel came into the army as a private and rose through the ranks to captain. Even though he was running track, many times the army never gave him a break," according to Phillip Schnnick, an air force track team member who traveled around the world with Pender. "At one time, he was in charge of recruits throughout Georgia, during the whole time he was competing.

"As an air force captain back then, I can tell you the more successful you were in your assignment, the more the military put on you in responsible situations. Mel had to work his a—— off and at the same time train. Back then, Mel was under a lot of pressure. He had to turn that key on inside of himself to compete, amid so much pressure. He was looked

upon as representing all African Americans in his position in the military. This was during one of the most racist times in American history!

"Mel was gifted with a great, powerful physique. He was like a fire hydrant, and many in our sport thought that was what made him so successful, but it was not. As a competitor, I can tell you that you cannot be tense and successful in track. A lot of athletes have strength, but they end up hurting themselves because they are not relaxed and concentrated on the task before them. Mel had a knack of coming through in competition.

"Most of Mel's success came from his mind. Too many people think because you have black skin you can run fast and do athletic things. Mel had a thing that goes beyond the mind, and it's good spirit, and that's what he had. It's a soulful thing.

If anyone wants to compete as a world-class athlete, all of the natural creative universal forces of gravity, time, weather, and temperature come together for you, and you become a commander within the universe—it is a spiritual dimension.

"Mel is still being honored around the world. Mel, Charlie Green, and I were in France, Greece, Ireland, and Cuba in competition, and he is still remembered. I was in Cuba about three or four years ago, doing some United States-Cuba relations friendship stuff, and there, the contributions of Mel Pender are immortalized on a massive poster at the airport, at the home of someone he competed against years ago. In fact, knowing Mel, serving as chairman of Athletes United for Peace, and being an athlete helped me to get the right connections so that I could leave the country and return home.

"I had run out of cash, and credit cards were not in place in Cuba. I ended up going to a funeral, and there were fans who could give a play-by-play description of the exchanges in competition during a Cuban relay involving Pender. The order for the relay was Herme Ramirez, first leg; second leg, Juan Morales; Pablo Mundo Green was third facing Pender, and last was Figerola Hines. Mundo died of a heart attack, and, it was Morales who had the large photo in his house." Dr. Phillip Shinnick is director of the Research Institute of Global Physiology, Behavior and chairman of Athletes United for Peace.

"I was a military man who ran track. I was in the air force. Mel and I got to know each other in Norfolk, Virginia, during a training

camp as different branches of the military would train in anticipation of track meets in Europe. I think that was in 1967.

"What amazed me then, and now, is that he didn't start running until he was twenty-three or twenty-four years old. As an athlete, it gave me a great deal of inspiration. When he saw a barrier, it did not matter, he would really go after it, and I loved him for that. In the face of overwhelming odds and obstacles, he has maintained a very upbeat and positive attitude. A lot of Olympians have fallen on hard times, and Mel has become an advocate for them.

"Jim Hines, who claims to be first sprinter to break 100 in the 100-yard dash, was living on streets in Oakland, California. The Olympics Committee has a slush fund they can use to give temporary funds to help those in need, and he has worked for the proper and timely distribution of them. Recently, he came out the stands at a meet in Sacramento, California, to inquire about the well-being of one of the country's top high jumpers in the 1960s, Gene Johnson. Harry McCalla, of the US Air Force and the Forty-Niners Track Club, traveled the world with Pender

"Little did I know, when I was twenty-two, I would see him while I was running track for the army an all-services track meet in Fort Belvoir, Virginia. I was stationed with H. Company, First battalion, Third Brigade in Fort Lee, Virginia. I didn't get to challenge him on the track because he was coaching the track team from the West Point Academy. I made my way to him and was prepared to salute him, even as second lieutenant I was not required, and he said, 'You're little Jackson from Lynwood Park.' That was one of the greatest days in my life. With his status, I felt real proud. I would see him years later as a businessman who operated a sporting goods shoe store at South DeKalb Mall. Now, I see him at times on the golf course." Johnny Jackson, retired chief orthoptist/prosthetist of the Atlanta Veterans Administration Medical Center

Chapter 15

Facing Enemies, Finding Jesus

Vietnam age 31

Once our unit settled in, it was time to start looking for "Charlie"—that is what we called the enemy, Vietcong (VC). Prior to going out, Rod and I experienced our first causality. PFC Marvin Manternach lost his life right outside of the base camp when he stepped on a land mine. It scared me. I had been close to death before but never had seen it firsthand. Reality began to set in, and all my training had brought me to this place.

Our first three days out were hell, to say the least. We had to travel through some heavy terrain, and one of my men chopped his knee open with his machete. He had to be airlifted by helicopter to get medical attention. One night it poured down rain. None of us were prepared for how cold it could get when it rained. We dug and set out explosive claymore mines.

The men were so scared. I couldn't sleep at all. Concerned for the men's safety, I was up several times checking on them.

In war, maybe more than at any other time in your life, the words "Lord, have mercy!" and "Jesus Christ" are not just expressions. They are pleas of hope and faith, whether you want to admit you believe in a higher power greater than the M16 in your hand, or the explosiveness and the grenades in your coat pocket, or not. That is because war is indeed as close to hell as anyone should want to get. You are scared, whether you want to admit it or not.

You do wonder if one day, or night, might be the last one you are heard from on earth.

You wonder how your family is doing. You think about your life and what you've done to enhance or damage it. If you have loved ones, you wonder if you'll ever get the chance again to tell them how much you love them. All kinds of things emerge, and you have to put them aside and remember your mission and your training—and do your best to stay alive.

One night, one of my men standing outside the foxhole was smoking. He was doing so without considering that it would signal our presence, and location, to the enemy. I flipped out, and I was livid when I saw him. It took strength not to shoot him myself since he had put us all in a dangerous position. If the VC smelled the smoke or saw him, we could all have been killed, and someone else would be writing about this incident.

Near-death situations in life have a way of making you think about and rethink your beliefs in God and your life in general. I know we all feel invincible at times and that we will be here forever, especially if you are young men like men back then. I felt as if I had some kind of coat of armor around me, but young men and women die just as easily and now as frequently as aging seniors. Then, and now, it did not take too much for me to understand that I had to cling to God's unchanging hand and remember all the religious teachings I had ever received and try to live by them.

Well, my platoon sergeant liked the offending young man and stood up for him. I wanted him out of my unit. We had trained the men well, and he should have known better. It took the whole night for me to cool down. By morning, we were moving to our next position.

The 9th Division was responsible for security on the Mekong Delta. The Mekong Delta is in the southern part of Vietnam. It is a huge maze of rivers and swamps with rice paddies and villages. Part of the 9th assignment was to ride with the men who drove the river-boats. At first, my men thought this was fun since they didn't have to walk. However, it was not so much fun when the VC started shooting at us like sitting ducks. Right there in the middle of the river.

Some things will never leave you, and I will never forget the day one of my fellow officers was killed. The VC was waiting for his platoon along the river and ambushed them. I will not detail what they did to those soldiers. It was horrific. I must have cried for two days straight. My heart went out to his young wife and children. She had just had twin boys. We had spent time together in OCS and Fort Riley. When our comrades were killed, it seemed like everyone changed. All the men became angry and were ready to kill anything.

No matter how you were raised and no matter what you are taught in church, an unbelievable change came over all of us. The men were not the same since. I too changed. It is hard, even today, to find a Vietnam veteran who can easily talk about the horrors they experienced in that war. The truth is that war changes everyone, and as time has proven, the war in Vietnam took a huge toll on my generation.

Posttraumatic distress syndrome (PTDS) is real.

Agent Orange victims are real.

Vietnam

I am a victim of Agent Orange. Agent Orange is a term for a chemical that was sprayed on foliage in Vietnam. Recently, my doctors advised that my battle with prostate cancer most certainly had come from Agent Orange. Later on in my life, doctors discovered that I had CLL, a slow-growing leukemia. I still have CLL, and it is being monitored by a cancer specialist. I have a different perspective on life after going through all this and knowing that it can strike anyone at any time. Remember, we are not promised tomorrow, so we must be careful how we live today.

I went on another mission, and when we finally returned to our base camp, I was met at the entrance and told by another officer that I was returning to the United States. He did not know why, and neither did I, but I sure was eager to find out.

Later that evening while playing poker with some of the other officers, which was something we regularly did, I saw LTC Chamberlain walking through to take a shower. I stopped him and asked him if it was true that I was going back home. He responded that I was to report to his office the next morning at eight o'clock and then I would find out.

I talked with my buddy Rod Morris. "If I had [your] speed I'd be leaving the country [Vietnam] and I would leave the fighting to guys who were not as fast," recalls Morris, who now makes his home in Florida. The next morning, I was on time. LTC Chamberlain told me that I was being sent back to train for the 1968 Olympics. I was full of mixed emotions. Leaving my men was very difficult. They were my family and my responsibility. I was committed to keeping them safe and getting them back to their families in one piece. On the other hand, that competitive spirit in me wanted to have the chance to win the gold medal that eluded me in the 1964 Olympic Games. Ultimately, the decision was not mine to make. There was no choice. The army's sports bureau in Washington had ordered my return. Like I said before, when you join the military, you belong to the army, lock, stock, and gun barrel.

A note about Second Lieutenant Rod Morris—we became friends prior to Vietnam. I met Rod at Fort Riley, Kansas, when he approached me to play on the football team. His first question to me was if I ever played tackle football and my response was "No.". I lied because I was too busy training my men. However, later I told him that I had played both in high school and in the military and that I had five NFL contract offers. He reminded me that I was a track star and he was looking for someone fast. His next statement was, "Don't worry, I'll coach you." He just wouldn't accept a *no* because the orders had come from Colonel Kufman to put this team together. Being a polite Southern officer, I said, "Yes, sir," giving him a great smile.

I was his second player picked for the team. This team must have been really important to Colonel Kufman because while we were conducting tactical training operations, the colonel authorized his personal helicopter to pick up all of us on the football team and flew us back to the garrison. The colonel was there to watch our first practice, and afterward, we were flown back to our units to continue our training. Both Rod and I thought this was funny, but we did feel very special. My boss just shook his head over the whole ordeal. This was the beginning of a lifelong friendship between Rod and me.

After leaving Vietnam, I was sent to Fort Sam in Houston, Texas. I was on top of the world when I was running. The track team at Fort Sam was made up of all new runners. I knew only a handful of them. When I was in Vietnam, I had thought my running days were over, so I really did not think it was for the army track team. I really believe that God has always had a specific mission for all of us, and in my case, he was giving me yet another opportunity to chase after my dreams. He was not finished with me yet.

Chapter 16

The 1960s: A Decade for Hope

"You must be the change you see in the world"
Mahatma Gandhi

For me, and I believe many others, the 1960s encompassed a decade of hope. Not just hope alone, but hope and drive to urge a country to live up to its creed of equality, freedom, justice, and liberty for all. Powerful acts of sacrifice, defiance, courage, and cooperation made a lasting impact on America and the world. There were events throughout the 1960s that had their own way of emphasizing on our nation's beliefs. I am convinced our military, sports, the arts, and enlightened political leadership turned the hopes of many of us into realities despite what initially seemed like insurmountable odds.

Successes in almost all endeavors resulted from people of all races and colors working together for a common good. Thus when America needed to put on a good face for the world at the 1964 Olympics, the parade of athletes from this country reflected the population of this country. I was twenty-seven at the time, and it was my first Olympics. I was the oldest sprinter that ever ran in the

Olympics. Many in the media discounted me as being too old. Well, the so-called experts, along with some competitors in track, soon would discover that age, for me, was just a number.

Outside of the military, the 1960s was like looking at a suspenseful, gripping, movie in which you hoped the good guys would emerge as victors. Sometimes they did. Too often they did not. Ironically, the events that filled the 1960s were in response to public pronouncements regarding racial ideological shifts. As a solider, I was engaged in military combat in a war, the likes of which our country had never faced before.

Our efforts in Vietnam did not resemble what my country had just engaged in the country of Korea. Our enemies in Vietnam were not clearly identified like they were in Korea. They often looked a lot like the civilians we went there to protect and uplift. Some of the villagers, who helped us in one setting, easily could transform into a Vietcong combatant in another, all within the same day, or week. Hundreds of black soldiers were on the front line in our country's efforts to bring democracy to a country where armed communist military leaders in one part of the country wanted to dictate life for all Vietnamese.

Holding on to My Dream Dodging Bullets, Bigotry

The contributions of many civil rights icons like the Rev. Dr. Martin Luther King Jr., Thurgood Marshall, Jackie Robinson, A. Phillip Randolph, Mahalia Jackson, United Nations Ambassador Andrew Young, Congressman John Lewis, Ruby Dee, Julian Bond, Mary McCloud Bethune, Congresswoman Barbara Jordan, Harry Belafonte, Arthur Ashe, Althea Gibson, Muhammad Ali, Ambassador Theodore Britton, and Jesse Owens are well documented. I can't add anything new to their accomplishments or a host of others. I can say I am better for meeting many of them, including Olympics hero Jesse Owens. What I can do is tell you about how some of us in the category of firsts—who entered into once-segregated settings, found ourselves facing challenges. Many people cannot imagine, and may not even believe or want to believe the hurdles of racism. I had to negotiate. I am only going to discuss a few of them. God made our blood one color, not black, brown, yellow or white—just red. Segregation still exits. Fear and hatred of other races is still being taught, but not blatantly. When it occurs though, it feeds racism.

Meanwhile, with our homes in foxholes and military tents, we did not have access to daily offerings of news. I was void of many of the events stateside. Oh, I had heard things, but we were so far away and we were fairly busy staying alive. When we heard of events from back home, it was through letters or from soldiers coming in for a tour of duty. Our country dodged a nationwide bullet with our involvement in Vietnam.

When the US Supreme Court decided that educating children should be open to all young people and free of unequal segregated setting, the floodgates to equality for all Americans were opened. Remember how the water does when a rock is thrown in to skip water, it creates ripples. It seems to me, that is what the 1954 Supreme Court school desegregation decision did. It gave black people a tool in the form of a ruling that provided hope, and they took it from there.

Back on Feb. 1, 1960, college students launched sit-in demonstrations at the Woolworth store lunch counters in Greensboro, North Carolina. Once word began to spread, similar protests were held in fifty other cities nationwide. In Alabama, students protesting at the state capitol heard the threat by the then-governor: "Someone is likely to get killed." Elsewhere, there came wade-ins at beaches, kneel-ins at churches, Freedom Rides began in 1961, testing public accommodations. At every turn, white bigots often showed up to torment the demonstrators violently, and sometimes fatally. Peaceful, nonviolent civil disobedience became the rule of the day rather than the exception. Every racial wrong imaginable was being challenged. Both blacks and whites were among those protesting. There were massive public demonstrations involving both blacks and whites. One involved some two-hundred-thousand-plus protestors in the 1963 March on Washington. It was at that protest in which Dr. Martin Luther King Jr. gave his famous "I Have a Dream" brotherhood speech. At the same time, many whites resisted desegregation through violence, and some in the South even used the Bible to defend and justify their hatred and actions. They cited the second half of Exodus 33:16, "So shall we be separated, I and thy people, from all the people that are upon the face of the earth..." and the second half of Leviticus 20:24, reading, "I am the Lord thy God, which have separated you from other people."

Under the color of state laws and some national laws, African Americans were discriminated against in their use of public facilities, denied the right to vote, and generally relegated to second-class citizenship. The military was one of the first places where the hope of equality and justice was practiced by the promotion of soldiers based on abilities, rather than race. If you met clear, fixed requirements, there was a good chance if would be hard to deny that promotion.

Before he was assassinated, President John F. Kennedy embraced the Civil Rights Movement and its leader, Dr. King. Kennedy announced he would send legislation to congress to address the racial turmoil that had engulfed our nation, especially voting rights. In some Southern states, only blacks were required to pay poll taxes and pass tests before they could vote. He did not live to see the fruits of his labor. President Kennedy was assassinated in 1963. President Lyndon B. Johnson was given the task of trying to right the many wrongs blacks within the Civil Rights Movement tried to correct. His actions helped greatly as he marshaled through the Voting Rights Act and presided over the Fair Housing Act.

Our other support came from foot soldiers who marched for freedom, equality, and justice. The many events that took place during the 1960s emboldened individuals to stand alone sometimes and in groups at other times. This 1960s decade was filled with blood in the streets. After President Kennedy was assassinated; Dr. King was killed; Kennedy's brother, Robert, a United States senator seeking the office of president, was killed; Muslim leader Malcolm X was gunned down; civil rights activists were the victims of senseless murders trying to get blacks registered to vote and exercise their rights; demonstrators were attacked during peaceful nonviolent protests—and many still carry those scars today. Some of the victims were former soldiers, like me. One was in my own state, about sixty miles from where I once lived—Army Reserve Lieutenant Colonel Lemuel Penn, who worked to register voters with the National Association for the Advancement of Colored People (NAACP), was ambushed and killed. A white housewife and Unitarian layperson from Detroit, Viola Luizzo; James Reeb, a Unitarian minister; Jimmy Lee Jackson, a Baptist deacon; and Johnathan Daniels, a seminarian also were among those who lost their lives in Alabama, volunteering in helping to get blacks registered to vote.

In the foxholes of my Vietnam tours, I would lie there at night wondering if Americans at home really knew what they were fighting for. We were the good guys. Some of us were black knights, coming in and fighting for all people regardless of race or religion. Yet when my fellow black soldiers and I returned to America, we were treated as second-class citizens, "baby killers." Why? I can't begin to tell you how much that hurt. In the jungles of Vietnam, we were soldiers (both black and white) who fought and died together as one. My heart ached for every soldier who was injured or killed. My troops were American soldiers, not black or white soldiers. These are some of the many things, as an African American soldier and an Olympian, that I had to think about while I was in combat in the military. There is no real need for me to rehash what already is in our nation's history books. My voice is about the remainder of the story that is not so well-known. I was part of that.

Soldiers in the military had sense enough to know that whatever was taking place in civilian life was not something we could embrace physically, no matter how much we felt about it emotionally. This is strongly implied in the oath of service we took to defend our country—right or wrong. Safeguards are in place to maintain discipline in our army by punishing soldiers for disobeying direct orders and violating our oath of service. Well, as a soldier on the campus of San Diego State University before the 1968 Olympics, I was around Professor Harry Edwards, a well-known civil right activist. He helped to plant the seeds of protest by athletes and others on campus.

The troubles I experienced at West Point came after the events of the 1968 Olympics. Our nation was in a cold war with our archenemy then, Russia, and America's problems with the issue of race was part of the propaganda used by our country's enemies to point out the nation's hypocrisy when it came to the issues of freedom, equality, equal rights, and justice.

A clenched fist, raised chin-high or high above the head, became a symbol of black power and black pride. In many ways, to some it symbolized a departure from the nonviolent demonstrations that had produced so much change for black America. Instead, I believe it started to generate fear. Meanwhile, on my immediate front in the military, winning the Inner Service Championship put me in the 1968 Olympic trials in Los Angeles, California. I don't remember much about the Los Angeles trials, all I know is that I placed third and I got the opportunity to go to Lake Tahoe, California.

Lake Tahoe training facilities 1968

Lake Tahoe's scenery was beautiful. We were on the mountain in the woods, and our track was placed there just for the trials. There were trees everywhere. Tall pines surrounded the track, and when we ran, we could not see around the track for the trees. Lake Tahoe was a perfect place for us to train for altitude. We were at 7,300 feet above sea level and Mexico City was about the distance. It was imperative that we had to get used to the air quality if we were going to win. There were a couple of guys that tried to train to run fast, but they got sick and were disqualified.

Our living quarters were primitive, small trailers with no showers. There was no comfort to say the least. We had a community shower, and you can imagine what it was like with a bunch of sweaty athletes having to share it. Our wives joined us about the second week there, and we had to rent apartments. The Amateur Athletics Union's allotment for living expenses was only $2 a day. That was not going to pay for anything, so many of us had to take on extra jobs. I was fortunate to have my army pay; many guys didn't have anything to fall back on, and they were in hardship there. One of the schools in the community gave me work too, so I was okay financially.

Chapter 17

Viva, Mexico

Upon our arrival in Mexico City, we saw soldiers with guns. This was amazing to all of us. We had no idea that there had been any trouble there. We were loaded onto buses for the Olympic Village. Our route was through the city, and what we saw were buildings that had been painted bright red, blue, green, and yellow. The whole area of the route had been cleaned up. We asked the police what was going on. They explained there had been a lot of demonstrations by the college students, and many people had been killed. The military had relocated what remained of the people—some to the nearby mountains, and we were told others were held in jail. They had to do a massive cleanup in a very short time.

I'd been to Mexico prior to the Olympics for the pretrials. The streets and buildings on the route to the Olympic Village were filthy and run-down. I learned a valuable economic lesson there. There were a lot of locals selling souvenirs on the street. We had passed by them on our way to the training camp. John Carlos knew I liked jewelry. I saw some, and he warned me not to buy it because it was cheap. I did not listen. I bought the nicest ring I could find, put it on, and the next morning, my finger was green. I spent good money for it too. Now, the way Carlos tells it, I bought a whole bunch of jewelry, and my whole body turned green. I won't ever live that one down.

Earlier, I mentioned Professor Harry Edwards of San Diego State University. At the time, he was a very influential educator. Edwards was planting seeds of change in the minds of every student, and black athlete, who would listen to his teachings. Tommy Smith and John Carlos grabbed a hold of Edwards's teaching, and they expressed some of it in the 1968 Olympics when they made a memorable, and courageous, protest during the playing of America's national anthem.

When Tommy and John finished first and third, respectively, in the 200-meter sprint, they entered the victory stand with black socks (to represent slavery and discrimination that blacks had suffered in America), and they wore Civil Rights buttons with medals around their necks. That was not all. As the national anthem was being played, instead of standing at attention, they stood with their heads bowed, raising one fist each. Smith raised his right arm and Carlos raised his left. Both hands were covered by black gloves. Back then, that had been dubbed the "Black Power" salute.

I can't imagine they knew the impact of their stance would have worldwide, but they had the faith to believe that their action would somehow effect change.

As Smith and Carlos stood there with their fists raised for freedom and equality, there was a whole host of black and white athletes behind them, united in the cause. Our team was irreplaceable and bonded together for life. None of us expected Tommy and John to do what they did; we were all in shock. This unrehearsed act of courage had a rippling effect around the world, and is still acclaimed today, even though, at the time, it would become a tool with which to punish us.

"People thought the victory stand was a hate message, but it wasn't. It was a cry for freedom," Smith maintains in the book *The Civil Rights Chronicles*, by Clayborn Carson.

My famous start photo

1968 Olympics 100 meter race

Smith and Carlos were suspended from the 1968 Olympic Village. The International Committee expressed its disapproval and immediately ordered Smith and Carlos to leave the Olympic Village for violating a basic principle of the Olympic Games—"that politics plays no part in them."

Smith and Carlos were not alone in protesting. Other athletes protested, but in different ways. For example, men like Lee Evans, Ron Freeman, Larry James, and Vincent Matthews, who comprised a relay team, showed support by wearing black tams. Before taking the victory stand after winning the 4-x-100 relay in record-setting time, I had Adidas make me a special pair of black track shoes trimmed in gold.

Avery Brundage, of Illinois, was the fifth president of the International Olympic Committee, and those of us who were black viewed him as a racist. Brundage referred to black male athletes as boys. "If those boys act up, I'm going to send them home…" was what he said publicly and privately.

When the black athletes heard about this, it was more than we could stand. Remember, in April of 1968, Dr. Martin Luther King was assassinated in Tennessee. We had to take a stand, so we gathered in the training room. and our head coach, Stan Wright. stood up for us. He called Brundage on the phone while we were there, telling him that we were not "boys," but rather men and that he was not to call us that again. Knowing how upset we were and how he needed us at full potential, his action and support defused us for the time being. However, Brundage's remarks brought our team of black and white athletes closer together and with an urge to make a statement with our performances the world would not forget. We were about to make the greatest mark on Olympic history, and our team had become such a cohesive force that no one could console us.

When Jesse Owens, the first black athlete to gain significant notoriety on the world's stage, won several gold medals in Germany, he was honored there; but when he came back to the United States, he was treated inhumanely. They had him showing his great speed and ability by racing horses. That is not how we chose to be honored or remembered. We had trained hard, given our time to the arena of sports; were acting as diplomats for our country, and we wanted to be recognized and treated with fairness and equality. After all, we needed good-paying contracts and jobs when the Olympics were over. We would do our part, and what we were asking for was that America to do its part.

I and others associated with the military were called in by a representative for the military athletes and, for about twenty minutes, were told we could not be part of the demonstrations based on the oath of service we took. Nevertheless, I wasn't going to back down, and somehow, some way, I would show my support. I knew that the times for black people were about to change, and there was no going back to what we knew. We would suffer for a time; some would die for the cause, but change would come. Those that were of the old school would have to lay down their fears. No longer would they lead; we were now the leaders.

My experience with Jesse Owens is one I will never forget. Young people of African American decent need to know something about their heritage—namely, where they have come from and who has helped to pave the way for their future. The Olympic Project for Human Rights, which was put in motion at San Diego State University, sought to bring the reality of our situation to the world, and set it straight. As a black military officer, I had firsthand experience as to what racism was all about. Both having grown up in the South and my military career gave me that awareness. I was in full support of this movement even though I couldn't physically do much. Although I had sworn allegiance to the United States Military, the movement was very much a part of who I was, and my support of it was in the heart of every encouraging word I gave to others that were active in the struggle.

There were meetings every night with the black athletes, both women and men. We were organizing ourselves, and each person had to make a decision as to what role they would play and how they would represent themselves. I was chosen as their spokesperson along with Ralph Boston. We were the two oldest athletes and were given that respect. People had a hard time making up their minds as to what they would do.

Brundage brought Jesse Owens there to talk us out of our plans. The problem with Owens was that he was not respected when he came back to the United States, and he never was able to make his success at the Olympics work for him. He was demeaned by racing with horses to show his speed and to earn extra money. Owens should have been on our side. He should have supported the cause since he himself was so poorly treated. To us, he was a spy for the white establishment and therefore had no place with us. We saw him as someone who had been sitting on the fifty-yard line with all the very important people, and he really had forgotten that he had been a struggling athlete at one time. He spoke to us as if he were Avery Brundage. Lee Evans said Owens was a confused man, and I do believe he was. Needless to say, we did not make Owens aware of anything we were planning and did not invite him to remain at our meeting. We carried on with our plans.

"The black fist is a meaningless symbol. When you open it, you have nothing but fingers—weak, empty fingers. The only time the black fist has significance is when there's money inside. There's where the power lies," Owens has been quoted as saying.

The 1968 Olympics has been recognized as the greatest ever with more gold medals won and more records set by the Americans. We reached our accomplishments without the use of performance-enhancing drugs, just natural strength, and the only high we had was from the blessings of God. As I think about this prestigious event—the beauty of the opening ceremony, how colorful it was, a stadium filled with people and millions more watching around the world—I can only say that there was no division between the black and white athletes. We were competitors on the same field, giving respect to each other for what we had accomplished with such great skills and perseverance. My mother came all the way from Georgia and joined me in Mexico. Words cannot explain what that meant to me.

Some of the people I grew up with in the Lynwood Park area tell me today how my presence in the 1964 and 1968 Olympics gave them pride. For many of them, no one they knew up close had ever done anything like what I was doing on a world stage. With my mother in attendance, I felt all their presence. I felt my Grandma

Wowa's presence too. In 1966, when I was training and traveling to Chile with the USA track and field team, Wowa was sick with cancer, and I had made a stop to see her at a hospital in Atlanta. I didn't want to leave her side, but she encouraged me to go on, saying simply, "You go ahead and win, I'll be just fine." She said it with that faint, but ever-present encouraging smile of hers. I left with those words, but not much comfort. Within two days, she had passed, and immediately I was flying back for her funeral.

My grandmother always said how proud she was of me and told everyone. I am just so glad she was able to see me grow up and watch me live my dreams. "That's my boy" still rang in my ears as I envisioned her presence here with me in Mexico. For that matter, I felt not only her spirit but the whole of Lynwood Park cheering me on. It was exhilarating.

Chapter 18

We Let Our Talents Talk

Once Olympic competition began in Mexico City, Americans in track and field dominated. Black athletes seemed especially driven. Sportscasters were linking our performances on the field with strides being made in America in the area of Civil Rights. Like it or not, we were cast in the role of athletic ambassadors, or black knights, at a time when the battle for racial equality was raging. Winning performances by American athletes were celebrated on every hand. In barbershops, restaurants, on television talk shows, and top ten radio stations. Sports, as I said earlier, have a way of making people see other people as athletes, not just black athletes or white or Asian or Hispanic—just athletes. Of course, we thought we had the best ones from America. In that Olympics, we did.

Talk about the actions of Smith and Carlos dominated the Olympics for days, but in the end, our performances took over, and boy did we perform. Members of the entire team for the United States were outstanding in heats and finals competition.

First up for me were the 100-meter heats. There were four altogether. The first three were qualifying rounds and then the finals. The goal was to place in the top four each time by running well enough to qualify for the finals over a two-day period. The 100 meters was my biggest event, and I had practiced hard and long to make it this far. I was told that I was too old to sprint and I would never make this Olympics. I guess I was being counted out early because my competitors had nothing to do but train for the competition we were in then, and I had to fly back and forth from whatever part of the country, or world, I found myself in as a combat soldier.

I proved them wrong even though I did not have the practice time as others. I had clearly kept in shape, and I seemed to pick up where I had left off. I have been told by experts that there is no one in the annals of track that overcame the challenges I had as a sprinter. I was a twenty-seven-year-old combat soldier, I was fighting in a war, and I was being shipped back and forth from life-threatening combat zones to the starting blocks all around the world. I cannot explain why I came in sixth place in the 1968 Olympics when the 100 meters was my best event. I could have won that race, and thought I should have. My start was great! I was out front, but it was like I lost all my momentum and fell way behind. Somehow I believe when people are really in your corner, you can fly above all circumstances. I did what I needed to do and then came the finals. I had a great start, and I was leading the race for about seventy meters. What happened next, I can't tell you? I felt I was on a winning pace, but when we crossed the tape, I found myself in sixth place. Ironically, at one time or another, I had beaten all those guys at least once before.

I did not have time to have a pity party; you never do in track. Elimination heats are run to get down to final competition. Two hours before the relay race, we exercised, jogged, warmed up, and then we got rubdowns. Then it was time to get your head together. In my case, I was thinking about getting out on the track to accept the baton and how I would negotiate the track for the first twenty meters. I kept telling myself, I've got to be out front. You see, I'm only five feet five inches tall, and I knew the other runners had an advantage over me in strides because of their height, so I knew I had to work on getting out of the starting blocks fast. Confidently, I knew nobody in the world could beat me taking off.

Later on, it was time. The 4-x-100 meter relay was called. The event was ballyhooed by every announcer associated with a television newscast. All kinds of speculations were on television and elsewhere. Remember, Tommy Smith and John Carlos had been suspended from the Olympic Village and could not compete, but there were speculators who wanted them on the relay team at the expense of those who were on the team. Some so-called experts were publicly suggesting the removal of Charlie Green because he had been injured, and I think they wanted me off because of my age and my sixth place finish in the 100-meter race. It did not help that in one meet leading up to the finals, our relay team came in second somewhere—I think it was in Canada. Many analysts and so-called experts thought we did not have a chance. I guess that is what started all the talk about us losing. We definitely had other plans.

Our coach, Stan Wright, was not supporting any changes to our relay team he apparently wanted in the 1968 Olympics. He expressed little concern about the injury to Charlie Green. Team members were united around Charlie 100 percent. We stayed by his side during his treatments and just stuck by his side, period. As a team, we were determined to run the relay together without any changes. The team had been practicing together for a long time and had a plan for victory that was working. Charlie usually started off; I came next because I was the fastest running on the straightway of the track, with Ronnie Ray and Jim Hines doing their best at the end. Back then, I recall that those in the race who were not 100-meter runners could not be substituted as they are in recent Olympics.

Precision and speed are the keys to winning the fast-paced relay. You've got ten meters in which you can't pass the baton, altogether you've got twenty meters in which it must be passed. The area is called the international zone. We practiced every day, sometimes twice a day.

I will tell everyone that there is no way you can say what anyone else can do, given the chance to try—especially in sports. Redemption was on my mind too, when the 1968 relay team lined up for the finals in the 4-x-100 meter race. I knew I could do better, and I thank God I got the chance to prove it. This was my last chance.

It was the 4-x-100 meter relay that I would find my wings once again and soar. I took my position on the oval track, awaiting the baton from leadoff man Charlie Green. Charlie ran the first leg, and when he handed the baton to me, we were trailing a bit. Passing the baton was clean. I was in a good lane; I think it was the third lane. It was without those curves that made you feel like you're running sideways. I ran the second leg, which proved to be the fastest of the four, and gave our team the lead. When I passed the baton to Ronnie Ray, he did his job, and we maintained the lead. When Ronnie Ray handed off the baton, Jim Hines brought it home.

We hugged and cried after the tape was crossed, and we won. We waved to our family and friends as they cheered for us. We jogged around the track and just celebrated. After toweling down, we were interviewed, and I remember one reporter asking why our team did not substitute for Charlie, and the answer came back: "He worked too hard to be left out of the opportunity facing him."

It was our moment in history to take the victory stand. It felt good to wear my special shoes that showed my statement of solidarity. How fitting for the moment. With each victory stand the black Americans took, there had been taken a step of courage, but the one most memorable was when John Carlos and Tommy Smith took theirs. Their black gloved fists were raised as a sign to the world that we had come from impoverished circumstances with heart and strength. Not just physical but mental and emotional strength to endure and overcome.

The ultimate experience caused me to wonder how we would be received when I got back. Would we receive the respect due? After all, my superior officers had treated me with such disdain and I was a combat soldier who won a gold medal in the Olympics. What did my family think? To my knowledge, the 1968 Olympic team has never been invited to or hailed at the White House like other Olympic athletes from other Olympic eras. Even the United States Olympic Committee made no effort to acknowledge the greatness of the 1968 team. Nevertheless, it was the greatest thrill of my life.

By now, everyone knows something about Tommy Smith and John Carlos. Here are some things about my gold medal teammates you may not know:

Charlie Green was my very closest friend. Originally from Seattle, Charlie and I met at the 1964 Olympic trials in New York. We ran against each other in the 100 meter, and Charlie got hurt. He didn't make the 1964 team, and I didn't meet up with him again until 1965. This was when we got to know each other better, and during that time, I suggested to Charlie that he join the army. He did, and then we joined together in the army track team to train. After Vietnam, I came back to California and Charlie and I trained together again both competing for the 1968 Olympic team. Charlie and I had grown to be very close friends, he was my brother. When you saw me, you saw Charlie, so it was fitting that Charlie's mother should join my mother for this great event. Adidas paid for our family villas, which was the only way our families could afford to join us. As I have stated before, we were a family playing poker at night for fun and running hard during the day. That was our life together, and we will never forget it. Today, when one of our teammates passes away, it is as if we have lost a brother or sister. This is just the way it is.

1968 Olympics 4x100 meter relay

Our relay team's victory walk 1968 Olympics

1968 Relay Team: Jim Hines, Charlie Green,
Mel Pender, Ronnie Ray Smith

Lee Evans was the middle child of seven. He had to help support his family by working the fields in California picking cotton and other crops.

Tommy Smith had a similar upbringing to Evans, with very poor living conditions.

John Carlos came from Harlem, New York, and Bob Beamon from Jamaica Queens. Both of them had it rough as inner-city black kids.

Beamon was a troubled youth raised by his grandparents. He had a choice of jail or the Police Athletic League, and school was of no interest to him. But to stay out of jail, he went to a school run by the Police Athletic League for troubled youth. Carlos, on the other hand, learned how to handle the streets as a kid. He worked for the family shoe repair business and learned to hustle on the side. I tell you this to say that none of us were born with silver spoons in our mouths. We had a gift, and we worked hard to get to the Olympics. We loved and respected each other because we all believed in the movement for change.

In my recent readings of Bob Hayes's life story, I learned more about what he went through during those times. Here, Bob was such a great athlete, yet he endured like the rest of us. I quote from his book, "Didn't matter the achievements or position it was strictly the color of your skin." Bob had signed with the Dallas Cowboys at the age of twenty-two, and part of his bonus was a $6,000 Buick Riviera. He was proud of his achievement and drove the car back to school in Tallahassee only to be harassed by the police at least once a week because a black youth just didn't possess such a car. Finally getting smart to the situation, Bob bought a black chauffeur's cap and put it on the backseat of the car so that when he would get pulled over from that point on, he could say that it was his boss's car.

In his book, Bob Hayes said, "We were allowed to entertain the masses with our talents, made our country the strongest in athletic achievements with more gold medals won, and yet we were still measured by the color of our skin. Well, it didn't stop us, we all were in this change together and God's will was done. America would know that we had arrived."

Phenomenal

"To accomplish what Mel Pender accomplished is phenomenal in the world of track. It is phenomenal that he made two Olympics track teams in 1964 and 1968, especially as a sprinter," declares 1968 gold medalist John Carlos.

"For him to do what he did at his age was exceptional! Mel was twenty-seven years old in 1964 and thirty-one in 1968. The competition we faced then was beyond world class, and everything he received is very much deserving. I was twenty, I think. We ran against each other in meets, and with each other in meets, all over the world. I don't know of many, or anyone, who accomplished what he did in that day and time in history.

"Mel also befriended me when I needed it as a newcomer, and those of us in the track community have established a powerful bond that has lasted over the years." John Carlos has been living in Ellenwood, Georgia, for the past three years. He is retired from working in education as a counselor in Palms Spring, California.

Majestical

"Mel was about seven years older than I was during our track competition. He, Ralph Boston, and William Davenport were like the fathers on the team. They were looked up to.

"Mel was majestical and always nattily attired in clothes without wrinkles of any kind. It was like perfection. He drove a clean 1964 or '65 Chevy with a 350 engine that I recall. When I first met Mel, he was on a college campus signing up ROTC (Reserve Officer Training Corps) members into military service.

We traveled together. He was flamboyant. I was quiet. Like a ruler, he was number 1, and I was number. 36. Mel has a personality of his own. He owns not only his footsteps but everybody else's. We shared many truths, and all of us developed strong friendships during, and after, the Olympic Games. We understand the backgrounds of each other, and we are still friends."

Tommy Smith is a 1968 gold medalist. He taught sociology at Oberlin College in Santa Monica, California for forty years before retiring. He now lives in Stone Mountain, Georgia.

I met Mel during the 1964 Olympic Games. Even though Mel was short in stature, most of us looked up to him. You never thought about his height. He was powerful and determined. He was older than most of the participants. I was nineteen. Mel and I helped to lay the foundation for the International Track Association and for male and female athletes to get paid in professional track events, once their amateur status ended. We were pioneers of professional track after the 1964 Olympics. I ran the 110 meters women's hurdles, and I was ranked sixteenth in the world. Then I think Mel was one of the top three sprinters in the world.

My professional career was as a sprinter. We ran as individual contractors. We had to win to realize a paycheck. We did not make much money then, but women and men were paid the same, $500 for first-place finishes, $250 for second, $100 for third with those finishing among the top six, another small amount. Now, with sponsors, track athletes can earn a living running, throwing, and jumping. I was the first woman to win. Our first meet was in 1973 at the Minidome on the campus of Idaho State University before 10,480 people, in Pocatello, Idaho. I was in good shape and beat both world-record-holding sprinters Wyomia Tyus (Simburg), and Barbara Ferrell in the 100 meters in 11.8 seconds. They were both out of shape then, but as soon as they got back in shape, they beat my butt. The ITA lasted three years, and the purses improved.

At the time, though, we had to come up with gimmicks to keep the public interested. We had challenge events featuring professionals from other sports, and there were battle of the sexes events, for example, which involved shot putter Bryan Oldfield, who would compete against women in runs." Lacey O'Neal is an international consultant and mediator in crisis management at the Department of Human Rights in the Superior Court of the District of Columbia.

"I met Mel during the 1964 Olympics, I was nineteen, I recall, and he was talking fast, as he does now. He always carried a smile. Many of memories fade over time, but like all of us then, he was a fierce competitor. Our time was one that just recently moved from being segregated, to desegregated. It always is good to see recognition come to those who have

made contributions to this country during some pretty perilous and trying times.

"If segregation had not limited our country so much, the field of competition in the Olympics would have been vastly different.

"As a product of the Tennessee State University's 'Tiger Bells' track team, my coach, Ed Temple would not have had to wait until 2015, to be honored. On August 28, 2015, the City of Nashville will honor him a statute memorializing his contributions. He has coached over twenty-three gold medal winners in a very short period of time and his players produced a 98 percent graduation rate. The good thing for him is he, like Mel Pender, is still alive to smell the flowers this nation should be giving them both.

"I know that Mel has given back to his country through his work with his community by coaching young people in track, I've been to some of the camps he had in Atlanta, and through his involvement with the professional International Track Association." Wyomia Tyus, of Griffin, Georgia, is now a retired instructor from the Los Angeles Unified School District where she worked mainly as a naturalist in outdoor education. Tyus was a gold medalist in both the 1964 and 1968 Olympics games. She won the 100 meters in both Olympics and was a part of a gold medal women's 4-x-100 relay team.

Chapter 19

Some of the Greatest

Receiving one of my medals from Ambassador Colby

My competition and travels around the world have brought me shoulder to shoulder with some of the greatest athletes from America and around the world. They include the following:

Ivory Crocket (fun, fast, and great friend), Charlie Green (great intimidator, superfast, and I loved him like a brother), Bob Hayes (my man, fastest man ever), Trent Jackson (funny), Gerald Tinker (talked trash, but could back it up), Dr. Delano Meriwether (strange and very mysterious, wore swimming suit with suspenders to run in), John Carlos (the man), Paul Drayton (genius, great friend, analyzed every race), John Moon (great teacher, taught me much about sprinting, and I owe him much), J. J. Jackson (high spirit, loved everyone, and a great friend), Warren Edmondson (all-around sprinter), Billie Gains (my little brother, fast and furious), Gerald Ashworth (great white hope), O. J. Simpson (cocky and talented), Ronnie Ray Smith (quiet and mysterious), Jim Hines (talented runner), Edwin Roberts from Trinidad (Latin Louie as we referred to him, funny and fast) and Lenox Miller (very quiet) from Jamaica, Tom Robinson (one of Bahamas's greatest, and a great friend), Harry Jerome (the fastest out of Canada), and Jean Louis Ravelomantisoa (the little man from Madagascar would surprise you). All these runners could have been Olympic champions—that is how good they were, and I have respect for them all.

The 1968 Olympics has been recognized as the greatest ever with more dozens and dozens of medals won and more records set by the Americans. We had no drug enhancements, just natural strength and the blessings of God with us.

Afterward

After all this, I returned home and had to take my mom to the doctor in Chamblee, Georgia. I knew something was wrong when Momma had us enter through the back door. The waiting room was segregated. Black people were told to wait in a little room that had two chairs and a little table far away from the front desk. We waited...and waited...and waited. I saw other patients, white, come in through the front door after we did and received service. I grew impatient and angrier. Here I was, an Olympic gold medalist, a combat soldier who risked my life for the United States, and I had to face prejudice and racism. I was fuming. *Why* does this have to be? I asked myself. That was enough. I went up to the counter to find out what was taking so long and why we had to sit in the back (which was like a little hole). The receptionist's reply was "That's where you people are supposed to sit." That was it, I hit the roof. Hearing me shout at a receptionist, my mom's doctor appeared, and we got into a verbal sparring match in which I told him off and listened to his threats of calling the police if we did not leave. By this time, my momma, fearing for my life, was crying and loudly urging me to take her home. I did, but not before I took my aggression out on my car steering wheel.

Once the 1968 Olympics ended, I thought I was headed to flight school to learn how to fly helicopters. At this point in my military career, I was Captain Mel Pender. Instead, they had me on orders to go right back to Vietnam. So what really happened? Well, remember I mentioned punishment for our victory stand gestures?

First of all, it is customary for the Olympic teams and medalists to be honored at the White House. That did not happen. Also, some team members received death threats at the games. Previously, I mentioned that all of the military athletes that participated in the Olympic Games were called into an office in the Olympic Village by a representative of the armed forces. He reminded us that as members of the armed forces, we could not participate in any form of demonstration. So, naturally, since I was not actively involved in any demonstration, I thought my plans for flight school were secure. I had taken and passed the test prior to the Olympics trials and all had been arranged for me to enter school. Originally, my training was to begin in September, but since I made the Olympic team, it was put off till February of 1969. So, you can imagine how I felt when I went back to Fort Mac Arthur and was handed orders to return to Vietnam. It was devastating.

I called Washington to complain, and I learned they had lost my records. In fact there were no records at all about my flight school test or my acceptance into flight school. I knew I was in the direct line of fire behind Tommy's and John's silent gesture and even though I had respected my position in the military and did not outwardly show my support as they had done, I was definitely being punished.

For the first time in my life, I wanted to quit, but the military wouldn't let me. I had lost faith in the one establishment that I felt should have supported me. Trying again, I was allowed to take the flight test over, but I missed passing by three points. I knew I was doomed, but God was on my side, and he worked it out. Before my second tour of Vietnam began, I was sent to Fort Bragg for six months and was made a company commander. Ironically, the same company, Charlie Company 325 in the 82nd Airborne Division was the same one I had been in as an enlisted man.

I was familiar with everything about this company—the buildings, the barracks—everything. Not only was I now a company commander, but I was the first African American captain to have a company. My company was first in every training exercise, every inspection, and my men were the most dedicated that I have ever served. We made our lights shine.

When my company flew from Fort Bragg to Korea for a training exercise, we parachuted in over the Hahn River in South Korea and I was the first one out. I led by example. The words I heard as a youngster came back to me: "Be the best." When I think back on that time, I realize that the army knew they had to do something to keep me in the military, and this was the only way: give him a company and let him be the first. My ratings were 100 percent the highest of anyone, and they would prove to be beneficial later on. It would be a miss to take all the credit for all of this since I too modeled after my commanding officer.

There is a time in life when you meet someone that you really admire and from whom you learn so much about leadership. This is what I experienced when I came under the leadership of Col. Ben Malcom my Battalion commander. He went beyond the call of duty in leading his men. His leadership and his demeanor made me want to be the best company commander and train my men to be their best. Col. Malcom served in both Korean and Vietnam wars, but the most impressive time in his career was when he was in Korea. His assigned duties in North Korea were like something you would see in a spy movie. Recently after reading his story "White Tigers-My Secret War in North Korea", I found an even deeper respect for him and can honestly say he's one I consider a real American hero.

After six months, I was shipped to Vietnam. I was there three months when I was sought out by Ambassador Colby, who was the CIA director. There was a position open. And because of my ratings and background, I was assigned to it.

Ambassador Colby had me flying all over Vietnam, Korea, and other parts of the Far East. Sometimes I flew on Air America, which were CIA-owned airplanes, and other times I had Korean pilots that flew one engine prop planes. These were scary and often we had to land in adverse situations. Not jumping out of planes or shooting at the enemy on the ground, this time I was coordinating the building of a park and swimming pool. Phantom Fun Park and the pool were built near the President's Palace in Saigon. I also coordinated the building of the tropical gym near the palace. The CIA kept me out there with the people as a goodwill ambassador working with the children in certain areas. This made America look good showing that we cared about their people and country. When traveling on the airplanes, I was courier for Ambassador Colby, transporting important documents to the different regions in Asia. Sometimes I would go on classified missions to Cambodia with the Special Forces. I was out on one of these missions and it really scared me because there were casualties. When I came back to my base camp and needed to touch base with home, I asked for ten days off, Colby gave me thirty.

Nine months later in 1970, I had orders once again to come back to the States and train for the 1972 Olympics. I was assigned to West Point Military Academy as the assistant track coach. Within three weeks, after being back, I was invited to run in the NAIA Championship and I won. While I was there I was asked to come to Richmond Virginia and run in the first indoor track and field meet against the Russians. I went and won. While there I was invited to Hamilton Ontario Canada to run. Again, I went and set a world record in the 50-yard dash. I say all of this to remind myself that it was really amazing to come from the jungles of Vietnam once again, with no training and accomplish all these victories on the track field. However, I ran in a meet in Seattle Washington twelve days before the trials for the Olympics and strained a muscle in my right calf. This affected my performance, and I wasn't able to make the team.

Chapter 20

Making History at West Point

Earlier, when I mentioned my desire to continue my education, I knew I had to have more. My first classes toward a college degree were at San Diego State University. Later, I was enrolled at Ohio University, Mount St. Mary's, and then on to Adelphi University, where I graduated in 1976 with a bachelor's degree in social science. I was thirty-eight. Since graduation, Adelphi has awarded me an honorary doctorate degree.

A healthy part of my college education came while I was basking in the glow of being the first African American assistant track coach at the West Point Military Academy. I can jokingly say now that I felt right at home because the nickname for the cadets is the Black Knights. To appreciate what this meant, the first African American cadet was admitted to West Point in 1870. His name was James Webster Smith of South Carolina. Henry O. Flipper of Georgia came later and was the first African American graduate in 1877. I was in the coaching neighborhood with some of the nation's best. Bobby Knight was coaching West Point's basketball team and Mike Krzyzewski played for the Knights and later coached the team. After helping my head coach, Coach Crowl, produce winning competitors, there was controversy when he passed away from a sudden heart attack and a replacement had to be named. I was named interim head coach and thought the job eventually would be mine. Bigotry reared its ugly head again in my life. One of my military superiors questioned my dating, which involved a woman who was not black. (At the time, for the record, I was single again with a daughter in college at Fisk University, in Tennessee. My first wife of eighteen years and I were formally divorced.) One letter in particular stood out in its reference to me:

"He was divorced once, almost married a girl who was not black...and then going around with another ...," the letter read. In other words, the author of the letter, and others, thought I was not a good family man.

Well, word got around to the cadets and they became furious. Some of them got up a petition unanimously recognizing me as their track coach and urged West Point to do the same. Officials at the school did not.

Here are excerpts from the letter to officials from Keith Simms, captain of the track team:

"At the time Mel was coaching, he was active Army, he was a decorated war veteran, he was still running in world class track meets breaking world records...our track team was one of the best in the East. Unlike our football or basketball teams, army track was well respected under the leadership of [Coaches] Crowell and Pender...After Coach Crowell passed away, a sudden flow of comments and rumors that I had never heard before were being floated that expressed concern that Mel had only just recently earned his BA (degree), that he was quite senior in age for a captain, that Mel did not have any command experience, and that Mel may not be a good example for the cadets. It incensed the track team because we had the utmost respect for Mel. We tried to identify the source, but never did, so we focused on putting out the real facts and squashing rumors. Cadets were initially surprised and puzzled that Mel was not immediately named as the new head coach. This later changed to a feeling of responsibility of the track team members to make certain that the chain of command was aware of Mel's [performance], and the team

accomplishments under his leadership by signing a unanimous petition from the track team..."

To my surprise, the track team did not stop with the petition. Simms told senior officers this: "When they announced that they were going to conduct a search for a new coach, it turned to shock and disappointment. Now, cadets are not allowed to protest, but in the *Army vs. Manhattan Outdoor Track Meet*, the team agreed to lose every event." The superintendent [at West Point], the commandant and many others in the chain of command were in attendance that day, and were quite taken aback by the lack of effort. Later on, in explaining to commanders why a national search was not necessary, Simms said he pointedly told commanders:

"Where else are you going to find a decorated war veteran, who was also an Olympic champion, a current world record holder and worked as an assistant with a track coaching legend in leading West Point to recognition as one of the most successful teams in the NCAA ever under their leadership.

"How could you find a better track coach?"

"You got me there," a senior officer replied.

The same officer said, speaking frankly, he did not think West Point was ready for a black head coach.

For the record, I was a company commander for six months with the 82nd Airborne Division and received a 100 percent rating. To make the facts straight, in Vietnam, I was a platoon leader and I was a company commander at Fort McArthur. So there should never have been any question of leadership or performance because I had received all high ratings.

There had been a so-called nationwide search for the head coach position; two black coaches were among the applicants. There first choice though was a white man who was a distant coach at William and Mary University. Once hired, he didn't last long, and Ron Basil, an African American, was eventually hired as the track team's head coach.

I was hurt to my core over the statement "not ready for a black coach." It was again that I would face an issue that involved the color of my skin and not the content of my character. The secretary of the army called me personally over this incident and offered his apologies. Although the damage had already been done, it did help me to know that someone from higher up was concerned about my welfare and was very disappointed on the things that had come to his attention. He said that after he had pulled all my records from Washington and saw what an excellent officer I was, he just couldn't understand why I hadn't been hired. I guess you could you say that this was another one of my *why* moments.

Motivator

"I met Mel, during my 1972 Plebe Summer, at West Point, when I tried out for the track team. Having been a high school track athlete and fan, I immediately knew who he was, from his Olympic and world record performances. But until that moment, I did not realize that he was an Army officer assigned to West Point. He was the first black officer that I had met to that point, and I later determined that there were only a few others. He stood out, not just because he was black, but because he was superbly well conditioned physically, which is important in that warrior institution, and more importantly he projected all the confidence, leadership and professionalism that would be expected of a professional soldier. That was an inspiring and uplifting first meeting, for this young West Point Plebe, because in 1972 there were relatively few black cadets and officers.

"In 1972, the army, and especially the old graduates and leadership, at West Point, were still adjusting and trying to find their way toward the acceptance of black cadets and officers. The West Point experience was designed to be very competitive and difficult for cadets, but it was also challenging, for the black officers stationed there. I observed Mel's positive attitude, courage, confidence, and absolute professionalism as he encountered discrimination and unnecessary doubts about his ability to lead, only because of the color of his skin.

"As the captain of the track team, my senior year, when Mel, was the interim head track coach, during a meeting with the commandant of West Point, a one star general, later to gain three stars, he said that West Point was not ready for a black head coach. Even to this day, that

was one of the most shocking and disappointing things I have ever heard at West Point, an institution that I grew to love. That statement went against all the excellent leadership training that I received there, during my four years. Not only was Mel a gold medal track Olympian, who was still competing and setting world records, the army track team, under Mel's leadership, had an exemplary and winning performance record. It still sickens me to hear from a general officer that work performance was secondary to skin color, in matters of deciding the promotions and career decisions, of those he was assigned to lead. Mel handled this situation with amazing grace, and the experience taught me that I too would meet similar challenges in my career and how to respond." Keith Sims, West Point, class of 1976 and captain of the outdoor track team. He now lives in the Atlanta area.

Winner

"I was incredibly impressed that we had someone of worldwide stature on our sports staff at West Point," says Mike Krzyzewski, best known as Coach K of NCAA national basketball champion Duke University Blue Devils.

"Mel certainly brought incredible credibility to army track, and also army athletics. He was always a gentleman and seemed to go out of his way to help the youngsters he had an honor to coach. They certainly benefitted greatly not just from his knowledge, but also from the fact he had accomplished at the very highest level in the world." Head Coach Mike Krzyzewski, Duke University Blue Devils men's basketball team who was at West Point during Mel Pender's tenure.

Friend

"I first met Mel Pender while we both were stationed at the U.S. Military Academy, West Point NY. Mel was the assistant track coach and I was a Clinical Specialist working at the hospital. Our first meeting is vague at this time but I most remember Mel always coming to the hospital to visit and check on cadets who were hospitalized. Not only did he visit with cadets who were on the track team but all cadets on the

wards. Much as he had done as a field soldier serving in line outfits and Vietnam, Mel shared a special relationship with all soldiers, officers, enlisted, and cadets. Much of this can be attributed to his having been an enlisted man before becoming an officer, but as I got to know him it was clear that it was the measure of the man that he was long before becoming a soldier. Mel was a loving caring person who shared a real concern for the welfare of others, sometime to a fault.

I do not know why nor how we bonded so quickly but we did and it is a friendship that has endured for over thirty five years. During that time I have come to know Mel up close and personally as well as his family and friends. It is when one is off the public stage that you really get to see and know the person and for most of our years our relationship has been away from the public arena. Later in my career I went on to become a management consultant and trainer and one of the stories I often shared with groups was the Mel Pender story. I referred to him then as my little SELF MADE MAN because he was the biggest little man I had ever known and had the biggest heart. While there were those who helped him along the way, the desire to succeed had to come from within. That is what impressed me most as I got to know him better. No matter what he got involved in, be it sports, business and yes, relationships he was going to give his all." William Hawkins, retired US Army lives with his wife Sally Hawkins on the Island of Dominica.

Chapter 21

New Way of Life

I mentioned to you previously that I was running professional track while at West Point. What I didn't mention is that my very last track meet was in Atlanta. It was such a great event and would set the stage for my professional life. The first black mayor of the city of Atlanta then was Maynard Jackson, and he was well liked by the community. The mayor, along with my high school principal L. A. Robinson, attended the meet. It was a sold-out event that brought in many people from Lynwood Park that knew me and other areas of Atlanta. It was such an honor for me to show off my talent since many had never seen me run in person. They showed me much love and respect through their applause and cheers. With all the excitement and joy I felt, I lost focus unfortunately and didn't win the meet. Gerald Tinker beat me by a hair, which we still laugh about today. My loss didn't seem to matter to the natives of Atlanta. Their hero had come home to them, and their pride was well displayed. After the track meet was all over, the mayor made a special presentation to me with the key to the city and named the day Mel Pender's Day.

Just think, this little guy who grew up poor and had never run track until age twenty-five had come home years later a sports celebrity who now held a completely different status in the community.

This experience touched me deeply and was another factor in my decision to retire from the army to Atlanta. I realized that there was opportunity here for a black man. The city was growing, and I had a chance to grow with it. When I weighed Los Angeles against Atlanta, I saw that LA had major issues developing with crime and huge traffic problems, yet Atlanta, in its growth, still had retained the smaller communities of which I had called home. The welcoming embrace I received was enough to say, "Come on home, son."

Things happened so fast in my life, and as always my transitions have been swift. So, just like my sprinting, I wasted no time in getting out of the starting blocks. My retirement came in June and then college graduation in August and immediately the next day I took charge of gathering up my things. That was it; I was done with New York, and along with my new wife, I made my way back to Atlanta the very next week. We arrived in Atlanta with a new vision of life and settled ourselves down in an apartment at Plymouth Colony Apartment Complex located outside of Atlanta. It took no time at all to roll up my sleeves and once again go to work. By November, I would open my first and only retail store. Work seemed the only way to escape the pain from my hurtful experience at West Point. The more I worked, the more my thoughts would be taken up by the excitement of putting a new project together.

How did I get the store open so fast? you may be thinking. I told you I'm good. Really though, it was when I was back at West Point that one of my protrack buddies, Olympian Marty Liquori and his associate Coach Jimmy Carnes, presented me the opportunity to buy a franchise called Athletic Attic. About six months prior to my retirement, they called me up and told me about this great store that was new to the market. They said it was a pioneer store for people like me who have a pioneer spirit. Being the only store of its kind at the time, it was spreading fast along the East Coast. Marty had given me a little inside information while I was still running track about it, and our previous conversation really had stuck in my mind.

At the time of their phone call though, I had also been toying with the idea of owning a Cadillac dealership, which was offered to me by the corporate office of General Motors. Reading the newspaper, I came upon the article where it spelled out the opportunity for minorities to own their own dealerships. This article struck my interest so much that I applied for a dealership. Corporate office approved my application, but now Jimmy and Marty's offer of a franchise with Athletic Attic had given me two options for working after my retirement. Hindsight says that I should have taken the dealership since they still are around today, but my love of sports and the name I made in track led me to make the decision to break ground with Athletic Attic. It would be exciting, not to mention a way to express who I was within the confines of business.

Choosing the location was challenging since in 1976 there was still a great division between black and white. However, I would find myself in the middle of changing the way business was done. I became one of the first African Americans to own and operate a franchise store located in one of the major malls in Atlanta. I had narrowed my search down to two locations, the Perimeter Mall and South DeKalb Mall. Since Perimeter Mall was not as popular as South DeKalb Mall, my natural instinct was to go with the most shopped area, regardless of the future. Already, there were only white folks owning and operating retail stores in the malls, so it would be a challenge for me to break the mold.

It Does Not Hurt to Know Good People

When I approached South DeKalb Mall's management, I was met with resistance. They did not want to give me a prime location as I had asked but rather wanted to stick my store in the back, where they considered that section an outlet location. This didn't sit well with me at all and I demanded a better site. Needing some assistance to get the job done, I called on DeKalb County Commissioner Liane Levetan, the first female elected to the commission, came to my rescue. She did some strong negotiating with the mall's management, and when she was done, I was in a prime position and had a good agreement. The commissioner and I found common ground and stayed friends through the years, supporting each other in politics and different community functions. I even worked on her campaign to become the county's first female commission chairperson.

Carry on Mel Pender

Reconnecting and making new friends in Atlanta was not a problem for me. I love people, and so over the course of my military career, I have had to learn how to win friends and influence people on many different levels and in different ethnic groups. While my store was a large undertaking and it would require my undivided attention, it would quickly become a successful venture.

I worked fast from the time I signed the lease with the mall to the day of the store's grand opening. What a proud moment that was when the doors were open for business that first day. The store was painted in lots of colors. Shoes and clothing were carefully arranged as to provide eye appeal and salability. In other words, the store was beautiful, and it drew many customers. Shortly after opening, I knew I was going to need more help to serve all my new customers. Well, I got up at the crack of dawn and drove to the store, worked hard all day, then finally arrived back at home when the sun went down. I would repeat my routine day after day in operating a small business. This brings us back to the question of hired help. Well, I handled it.

It was Little Cynth, as I call her to this day, who I had been introduced to through her soccer coach, who would fill my need for an employee. She was an exceptionally bright and talented young soccer player (and a fantastic artist as I would later come to find out). At fifteen years old and in need of a summer job, Cynthia was a great candidate for employment at the store. I immediately hired her. She exhibited a lot of responsibility for her age and had a go-getting personality.

Not long after hiring Cynth for sales, I made her my manager. You can imagine how this freed me up to do some other things besides the store. I had someone who was likeable with customer appeal, and most of all, I could trust her. Since her first job with me, Cynthia has gone on to owning her own design and marketing business, which she has been doing for the past twenty some years. My, how time goes!

Because of my freed-up time, I was able to take on other projects.

In the retail business, you become connected to suppliers, and one of mine was Mitre Sports from England. Mitre had an office in Atlanta and one day their marketing director, Aris Akubian, visited my store. He was highly impressed and saw that I was innovative and skilled. He asked me if I would like to come and work for Mitre. He offered me a position in marketing and public relations and asked me to design a track shoe. My immediate response was *yes*! This again was a first, the first ever track shoe for Mitre sports who had been the number 1 company that carried soccer shoes and balls. I was really excited and felt it a great honor since I knew nothing about any of my fellow teammates being offered a similar opportunity by Adidas or Puma.

My time would be divided between spending it at the store and Mitre's corporate office. It would take about a year to design my first shoe. I started with a drawing that I had sketched on a piece of paper while I was thinking about what I liked and disliked in other shoes. I worked the sketch until it was perfect. Then we had to build the mold and work out additional details until we thought it would wow the market.

Mitre shoe advertisement

The track shoe was nostalgically named the Mexico, since that is where I won my gold medal. I was so proud when Houston McTear, the top sprinter in America at the time, wore my shoe. He set a world record in the sixty meters at Madison Square Garden and that gave the shoe even more clout. Creating the advertisement for the shoe was fun. I had my photograph taken on the steps of Bones, Atlanta's famous five-star restaurant while wearing a tuxedo and the track shoe. This became my marketing piece and was printed in newspapers and magazines. It also helped me put together a track club of all the top high school girls who ran track in Atlanta. There were twelve girls total and all wore my shoe. Muhammad Ali gave us his permission to name the track club after him, and now we were off to the races traveling all over the United States to different meets. The girls had never been anywhere out of the area before. We traveled to Kentucky,

Massachusetts, California and other places, meeting such superstars as Muhammed Ali, The Jackson Five and Marvin Gaye. The girls did really well always striving to be the best on and off the track.

While at our home meets, I would bring my company vehicle, which was a light-blue Chevy van with the Athletic Attic logo of a roof painted on both sides, and park it at the track. It attracted a lot of attention and was a great advertising tool. I used the van to carry supplies such as shoes, jogging suits, uniforms, and more which I sold at the track meets. With the use of my van, I always gained new customers, and it kept the shop busy.

I was multitasking long before techies gave the practice a name. While I was operating the store, managing the track team, and making shoes, I took on another program with the National Football League's Players Association. It was called the Vocational Expiration Program. Back when I was running pro track, I became a part of the union with the NFL, and they would use guys like me to run camps. I had run two camps prior to the NFL job, both were privately funded. My first camp was when I was still at the West Point Military Academy and when I retired to Atlanta, I did it in connection with the YMCA of Atlanta.

The NFL approached me to run what I still consider one of the most outstanding inspirational programs that shaped the lives of participants both young and old in such a positive way. From time to time, I take out the photo album and talk to anyone who is interested about how inspiring and life changing these camps were. With the help of many, the camp was put on for two summers, July 1980 and 1981. They lasted for two weeks at a time, and I loved it.

Anita Lee, who has served as a principal in the Atlanta Public Schools, was my assistant director, and she was good. She, along with a hardworking staff, kept the camp running smoothly. The whole concept of the camp was to involve inner city kids who were economically disadvantaged. They had to qualify through a federal program to get into the camp. We ran the camp like a town with a government and mayor. The campers had to run for election and be voted in. There was a store, bank, a TV and radio station, and we had people who were camp counselors but worked regular jobs with in these areas to spearhead them. They assigned the kids to each area to develop and run. Also, we had classes for those interested in art, nursing and photography. Lou Walker, a professional actor who played in *In the Heat of the Night*, came in to teach theater and those that had a gift for writing worked on the town's newspaper. The kids learned about the NFL union and how to be leaders in all areas of their lives. There were about two hundred kids per summer, and we had about forty camp counselors. The camp was held at West Georgia College in Carrolton, Georgia, where we lived in the dorms, and it lasted two weeks. What a great time it was.

Memories of the NFLPA Youth Development Camp Opportunity
Anita Marie Lee

> *The National Football League Players Association under the direction of Brigg Owens hired Mel Pender, as the director of the Atlanta National Football League Players' Association Program in Atlanta. Mel Pender provided the youth of Atlanta an opportunity to feel safe, secure, and a part of a unique family environment. Six hundred youth were transported to West Georgia College for an experience of a lifetime. The youngsters were in three groups of two hundred and attended one of three sessions for eleven days.*
>
> *I was hired by Mel as his assistant director, and I become the camp mother. Mel was the Father. He was the example of achievement, success—I CAN, and WILL ACHIEVE. He set the expectations for the participants and they rose to the occasion.*
>
> *Mel led by example, and because of his military background, we were up and moving at 6:30 a.m. There were very clear expectations of everyone. We all knew that everything was for, and about, the participants. This was during the crisis of the 'Missing*

and Murdered Children' and we wanted our youth to know that they were going to have a better future; because we were giving them an audacious opportunity of a lifetime. They were going to be treated as professionals, allowed to earn while they learned, and they were SAFE.

The participants were secure, protected, supervised, and taught to think for themselves, and their family unit. These youngsters came to us with pre-set ideas and left with a sense of unity, pride, and achievement. Our participants were empowered to learn and expand their horizons socially, emotionally, economically, and they knew that they could reach for the stars.

A micro society was established for them and they operated a government, police department, store, infirmary, human resource department, post office, fine arts, and cultural arts programs.

At the end of the eleven days our participants hailed Mel Pender as their HERO. They were in tears when it was time to return to Atlanta. During the follow up many of the participants called on Mel Pender to speak at their schools, to come by to see them, and to just be there for them. Mel fit the bill and they never forgot him.

I sincerely feel that all the participants left with more than they came with. They also endeared the staff and taught us a lot about life and living. They were our HEROES. They taught us to be more concerned, more responsible, and to always remember that we must be the village that will surround our youth.

Recently, I met up with one of the girls who had attended one my camps. She was now a grown-up and a lovely woman with her own family. Back then we called her Dimples because of the heavy indentation in her cheeks. She reflected with me and my wife of how the camp changed her whole outlook on life, and said she is grateful to this day to have come through the program.

Back to the sports store, we had reached record profits and along with the success came shoplifting. The real challenge was figuring out how to handle it. I remember one young man who worked at one of the shops down the hall. He would always come in, either on his break or after his shift was over. We would talk a while then he would be on his way. One day I noticed him to be different with his jacket zipped tight. My military training helped me to detect he had something under his jacket. Sadly, I realized it was one of my jogging suits. I didn't prosecute, sending him to jail or anything else, except give him a stern lecture, one I hoped he would never forget and I let him go. I just couldn't see a young person going to jail. I guess I have too big of a heart. Well, there were other shoplifters and there were other lectures, but I fared better than many stores, experiencing limited crime.

With the success of my store I was soon able to get a home for my new family within 3 years of the business being opened.

Chapter 22

Dream Home

I loved my new home in Marietta, Georgia and worked hard to make my yard picturesque along with the hard work I did on the inside of the house, it became fun for both my children and guests. My yard was completely bare, and I had to start from scratch, laying sod, planting flowering trees, bushes, boarders, and lots of beautiful flowers. That was a back-breaking job and one that would literally cause me pain for years to come. However, it was a good time for me to teach my son and godson, Charlie Webster, the value of work. I know they will never forget the lessons my yard taught them, and I will have lasting memories of it too. I lived in a predominantly white neighborhood, and the thought to some folks of a black man owning such a beautiful home and creating such a yard was hard to comprehend. I remember one day I had donned my white overhauls and proceeded to cut my grass on my riding lawnmower. I hadn't been long out there when a white couple pulled up in their car. They must have been impressed at the fine work I was doing because they asked me if they could hire me to do their lawn, not realizing that I lived there. Back then in the South, the affluent white folks still had "yard boys," and I guess they thought I was one. Even though the thinking of some had not evolved, the area was great for us to live and raise our family. It wouldn't be long after moving in that we would learn our neighbors and begin to socialize. I love to socialize with others, and it does not matter what color; however, the attitude does matter. For me, it was my dream home.

My home was like the homes about which I dreamed of owning when I saw them near the Capital City Country Club in my caddy days. We had a one-acre yard, and it required lots of work, but it brought lots of joy to the children.

My son, Javier, who was born within months after we moved in, was forever bringing home snakes and lizards. He was a true inquisitive boy who not only spent time outdoors but spent time in books learning about the things he discovered. I can honestly say that I put my heart and soul into this house along with that came the pride of ownership, and the compliments I received made it all worth the work. It was not just the fact that I loved my home, I loved my family who lived with me in this home.

We lived about a hundred yards away from a great fishing lake. It was about five acres and accessed only by those living in the neighborhood. I loved to take the children there to fish. The lake was stocked with bass, perch, and catfish, and that made it fun to see what we would catch. My daughter really got a kick out of the fishing.

"Daddy, Daddy, Daddy!" Melania would holler, every time a fish got on the line. She was such a tomboy. She is special and I am proud of her accomplishments today and the drive that she has. We spent ten years in the "dream house."

"Our lives begin to end the day we become silent about things that matter" Martin Luther King Jr.

Melania's baby picture

Javier's baby picture

Chapter 23

Changing Jobs

During a period I considered as a new lease on life, I was still operating my store and traveling around with the NFL Players Association speaking around the country. I spoke at Job Corps centers where I would give my motivational speeches to troubled youth who were learning a trade instead of going to jail. I was speaking in Albuquerque, New Mexico, at one of these Job Corps centers with some other retired football players when I met Les Shepherd. Les was a representative of the Home Builders Association who happened to be at the center for our presentation. He was impressed with my speech and approached me to find out if I might be interested in coming to work for them. He said that he would like to see me come to DC and interview for a position in my area. I really wasn't looking for a job at that time. My plate was full with a store, designing a shoe for Mitre, and traveling with the NFL; but I loved the idea of working with kids and, of course, the money sounded good. So after some thought, I made the trip to Washington for an interview. I was excited about the offer, which required travel, office out of my home, expense account, and salary that my store couldn't beat, not to mention that the benefit package was great for me and my family. I couldn't refuse, and so I took the job. Mind you, I still had the store and my commitment to the NFL Players Association. How would I work this one out? It took some time, exactly a year, and a buyer came for the store. What a relief, and my public speaking had decreased; now I could focus on my job.

The first year I was on the road three weeks out of the month. I had centers in South Carolina, Georgia, and Florida, which kept me hopping. After the first year of learning the territory, I narrowed my traveling to one week out of the month. This gave me more time for the family.

There were about eight hundred students per center, some had dropped out of school and were getting their Georgia Equivalency Diplomas (GEDs) and some had gotten into trouble with the law and were court ordered there. They all were to learn a trade such as carpentry, plumbing, electrical, solar energy, and apartment maintenance. I was responsible for about two hundred of these students, ensuring they were trained for the construction trades. Working with the directors of the centers, I oversaw the hiring practices of contractors in their region. It was also a big part of my job to build relationships between the contractors and the Job Corps centers. I would have to get to know them, their needs, and then find the proper student or students that could fill their job positions. Once hired, a student was no longer under the Job Corps but instead a full-fledged employee. It was rewarding to watch young people who have taken a different direction in life, finish a program that challenged their abilities and gave them self-confidence. To know that I was part of that process was truly the rewarding part.

All things do come to an end, and after ten years on the job, I found myself moving on. When I worked for the Home Builders Association, it was a time in America's corporate world when companies were given tax breaks for the hiring of women and minorities. It was the norm for the corporate world to hire one to three black men in upper management or key sales positions and then fulfill their quota with women, predominately white women. Then corporate America found that they could hire black women in those key positions, so there were fewer opportunities for black men to succeed in corporate America. My job was no exception to their rule. Within the Home Builders Association's upper management positions, there were three black men—me; Les Shepherd, my boss; and Landon Vernon, who ran another region. We were the only three throughout the whole of United States.

Eventually, I chose to move on, leaving the Home Builders Association behind me.

While I was with the Home Builders Association, I developed a great rapport with the Drug Enforcement Agency (DEA) and the Federal Bureau of Investigation (FBI). Representatives of the two agencies heard me speak to young people, and were impressed by my ability to motivate them. The Bible says that our gifts make room for us, and I guess my passion for children living clean and healthy lives opened up the doors for me to travel across Georgia, North Carolina, South Carolina, and Florida with the DEA and FBI to speak with even more youth. They paid me well, but that is not what drove me. It was the children. Seeing how my life story could make a difference in their lives, and encouraging them to make something of themselves, is what I enjoyed doing. When I looked back on my life without a father, seeing what I missed, I saw a little of me in many children, and it really made me want to help change their life's course. I thought about how going into the military changed me, and at every opportunity, I would present that to a wayward youth in hopes that they would choose this route. If it could change me, it could change them.

During my career with the Home Builders, I was able to be a father and family man. I gave time to my children, where with my first marriage and daughter I was unable to do that because of my commitment to the army. I wasn't at home then as I was now, which made all the difference in the world. This time, I didn't miss out on getting involved with the children's activities. Javier was in Scouts, and I helped out with making go-carts—you know I'm an expert at that—and occasional camping trips. He also played Little League baseball and football, and I found the time to coach one of his Little League football teams. Melania was in gymnastics and also spent a lot of her time with her cousin Eileen. My wife's brother didn't live far from us, and he had two children, Eileen and little Ralph. These two were together with Javier and Melania almost every weekend, either at our place or theirs. They loved each other like they were brother and sisters.

When I went out to speak locally at a school, frequently, my children would be with me. It was great education for them. I wanted to make sure they understood that they were no different than the rest of the kids out there; they just had it better than some because of my job. I wanted them to accept the differences of each other and to love all people regardless of race or economics. That is what my grandparents taught me and my church taught me growing up. It was my job to pass on my Christian beliefs that we were all made by God and that there shouldn't be any differences. I saw this as my duty as a father to pass this on to them.

At the end of my career with the Home Builders Association, I was honored with the highest award given by the FBI, the Hands that Work award, recognition of my natural gift to inspire and my deep spiritual commitment to fellowman.

There are some things about yourself that becomes clearly evident after similarly repeated experiences. The one thing that sticks out for me is that no matter how people wanted me to conform to their ways, and if it was not true to who I was, I just couldn't do it. They could never call me a sellout because it went against every principle that had been instilled in me from mother and father, grandparents and community of loving people. I saw that I have the power within myself to make choices, to know who I am and to be free!

When faced with these different yet similar situations, knowing this has kept me true to who I am and what I believe. The corporate world taught me about the climbing "corporate ladder," which often means the stepping on of one another, in order to get to the top. I found that you couldn't trust everyone, yet I still wanted too. What I saw and experienced hurt me, but I made every attempt to continue to impart to my children and the other children who heard me speak, they needed to have a clear understanding of people and how to be true to themselves.

This now brings me to an even greater challenge that I had to face, the loss of family as I had come to know it. The ending of a job

I could handle, but the end of my second marriage of thirteen years and the joy I experienced raising my children was something I was not prepared to see end. Now, a job, and a marriage was ending—so much for my "perfect world."

Mentor On and Off the Field

"I met Mr. Pender when I was seventeen years old in March of 1978 at a track and field clinic in Ponce, Puerto Rico, sponsored by Colgate Palmolive. The clinic was organized by Wilbur Ross, the author of The Hurdler's Bible. *Mr. Ross was a very precise type of individual and had an eye to detail and was good in identifying individuals that could become excellent hurdlers with their existing sprint speed. He attempted that with me, but I stuck to my 100, 200, and 400 events.*

"The clinic was comprised of Olympians and world-class athletes that included Ralph Boston, long jump and triple jump; Harrison Dillard, 110 high hurdles; Larry Shipp, 110 high hurdles; Madeline Manning Jackson, 800 meters; David Hemery (1968 gold medalist Olympian from England), 400 meter intermediate hurdles; and Mel Pender, sprints.

"I worked as an interpreter for Mr. Pender in the sprint group. As we went through the drills, I shared with my group all of his teachings and translated them into Spanish. Afterward, he was very impressed with how quickly I adopted his methods and saw that with my basic speed, I had the talent to improve. He told me that if I were to come back to the United States with him, he could have me improve to 10.5, 20.9. I was only running 11.3 to 11.5 on dirt, so, with all the advantages the US had with synthetic tracks, I trusted his words and believed him. Unfortunately, my mother would not allow me to leave although my father was very supportive of Mr. Pender's observations of my talent. In the end, my mother prevailed. However, shortly after the clinic concluded, he gifted me a pair of track shoes that he designed and told me to never give up and to keep applying myself. I had the only kind of shoes on the Island! They were white with a red letter M *in the middle. I had made a promise to myself to work even harder afterwards.*

"As I'm now fifty-four, I was very excited to meet Mr. Pender again via Facebook after all these years. I have had the good fortune to keep his philosophy near and dear to me as a public administrator for the Port Authority of New York and New Jersey and stay in touch and visit him. I'm very proud to see Mr. Pender again after thirty-seven years. His presence is a constant reminder of what excellence is all about. Win, lose, or draw, he instills that you must always be better than what you did yesterday, and you must get back up and try again. One must never quit. Mel Pender is a true champion and true fellow who has a zest for life. He is a champion across the board. He is not just an Olympian. I'm excited for him because he has been through hell and back. I can assure him with great pride that after all these years, it's been a whirlwind of a ride for me, but I've always managed to get back up and fight the good fight with faith in trust in Jesus Christ. Mr. Pender once mentored me, and now I have a young man I am mentoring, Graver Sandy, who went to the Pam-Am Games in July 2015. Jorge Mercardo, public administrator for the Port Authority of New York and New Jersey.

"I was born in Santa Ana, California, a short distance from Disneyland, in Anaheim, California. I attended Santa Ana Community College, in New Jersey, and as a freshman, I became national Amateur Athletics Union champion high jumper. The victory served to qualify me for the 1964 Olympics trials, and it was in New Jersey that I met Mr. Melvin Pender. I had never been out of Santa Ana. I didn't know anyone on the Olympics team, and I had to survive on the daily allotment of $2 per diem they gave us. It was clear to me that Mel could tell I, along with several of my teammates, were out of our elements. He took me and some of my guys with him to a PX (post exchange, which is something like Walmart, or Target but much more reasonable) to buy stuff while we were preparing for the 1964 Olympics. I bought some personal hygiene items, and my first battery-operated radio/record player. It was reddish brown, and I got one hit record being sung by Curtis Mayfield. I think it was "People Get Ready."

Mel will tell you that I could eat. I gained nine pounds even though I was in training, and I was not trying to do that. I ate all the food I could get during my meets. I would eat steak, fish, mashed potatoes, peas because at home, I felt I was doing good if I got two hot dogs and rice on the side.

All of my teammates loved what they were doing, but there was something special about Melvin Pender. He was older than all of us, and just having him with us competing was awesome. Pender was a man who was essentially, self-trained, and made the team at 27. Here was a man jumping out of planes, and facing combat in Vietnam, dodging bullets one month, and a few months later, waiting on a track starter to fire a gun to get him running down a cinder track, often to victory. I've always admired him for that.

Most sprinters who make Olympic teams are college trained, and in their early twenties. I had to retire at twenty-three, and my specialty was high jumping! Even though I was ranked as the number one high jumper in the world in 1967, I am the one who lost to Dick Fosbury in the 1968 Olympics with the unique backwards style of flopping that enabled him to run faster and then jump backwards, head first over the bar without knocking it off. I could not beat him during the Olympics, and came in second at seven feet, four inches, he jumped seven feet, four and a half inches—we met in other meets and traded places in who would come in first or second." Ed Carruthers, now a retired educator, was a 1968 Olympics silver medalist

A Hard Hit

Life has a way of throwing a curveball at you, and you really don't know how to handle it. Well, this was one moment in my life when I can honestly say I had that happen. My friends joked about how many times I've been married. Sometimes, I didn't know how to take it, but frankly speaking, I didn't care how they felt about it. It was said that I was a playboy because I dated a lot of attractive women, but being married early in life gave me little chance to date. Although I dated between marriages, my one true desire was to be a family man. With the marriage to my second wife, I felt that I was living that dream. I had a beautiful wife, wonderful children, and an absolutely gorgeous home.

I know that I may be repeating myself a little, but thinking back on my first wife, I knew we married young. All I wanted to do was work hard, make my family proud of me, and make a family with her. Putting all my effort into making her proud of me and my accomplishments only brought disappointment and heartache. She was not impressed by my success in the military or in track. The truth is we both grew up poor and had been given no chance to advance in life. Now, my second marriage was failing. We had represented an all-American family so well. It would become a shock to many, but that is the way some things are. You can't hide the truth; it will come out.

Somehow, we as a society still hold the belief that when we enter into a marriage, that we will honor our vows for life. God's help and strength are what a person needs to actually move on. I would come to find out just how much I needed my faith in Him. One of the most painful events in a person's life, and you are never prepared for it, is rejection. It is like a death of a loved one. Sometimes death sneaks up on you, and you never were given the chance to say goodbye. It leaves you struggling with emotions and unrest that you want to put to bed and shut the door, without God's help. Recovery from this takes years, and some people never recover. I just thank God for his mercy in my life and the fact that even though I got knocked down, I was able to get back up.

A short time later, a friend of mine who worked for the Georgia Tax Commissioner told me of a job vacancy with the Atlanta Hawks, National Basketball Association franchise. I didn't think I had a chance of getting the job since I wasn't a basketball player. He kept encouraging me, and I applied. Surprisingly, I was called for my first interview. It went well. A couple days later, I was called in for a second interview, which was more formal than the first. They made me an offer of half of what I was making with the Home Builders job.

"No!" was my reply.

The next day they called me back again and gave me a much better financial offer with great benefits. I became the president and director of community affairs for the Atlanta Hawks Foundation. The job title also came with a great office and lots of perks. My office was in downtown Atlanta in the CNN Center. It was impressive, and I was excited about my new position. It was clear that I had to be a multitasker. I was very excited about my new career, just the privilege of working for an NBA franchise after working with the NFL was an honor, and I didn't take it lightly.

When the City of Atlanta learned that I was a part of the Atlanta Hawks, I was receiving calls left and right to be on different boards. Serving the community was a part of my job description. Former President Jimmy Carter put me on the board of the Carter Foundation. Then-governor of Georgia, George Busbee, appointed me to the Bureau of Prisons Board and the Juvenile Justice board. After that, I was nominated to Hank Aaron's Rookie League board, the Special Olympics board, and a host of others.

When I served on some boards, I served as the Hawks' representative, and on others I worked to help to raise funds for the Hawks foundation. These funds raised would be returned to various community organizations. I can't begin to tell you how rewarding this position was to me. With the high-profile position came some public appearances, television interviews, and write-ups in local papers. I was the front man for the good deeds the Atlanta Hawks wished to portray. Each year I was actively involved in such fund-raising events as galas, fashion shows, and golf tournaments. I would have to employ staff and volunteers to each event, overseeing each project from start to finish. Sometimes the Hawks would ask me to supply them with entertainers for their halftime.

The main goal of the foundation was to help the youth in the community. I spoke at all the schools in and around Atlanta, bringing Harry the Hawk mascot and some Atlanta Hawks cheerleaders with me. Harry was a hit with the kids; he brought fun and they learned about clean living, their country and how to be patriotic in life as a whole. We put on one of the largest Stay in School programs in the country, by filling the Omni Arena with over five thousand students. This program had rippling effects in the NBA all across America.

In my first year on the job, I was in the role of a single dad, with my two children living with me full-time. They had a nanny to keep them when I was away for evening events, but mornings, I was there to dress them and see them off to school. Sunday nights I would iron all their clothes for the week, making sure we had everything in order. One of the things I dreaded doing though was Melania's hair in the morning. It was clear that I was not a hairdresser, and often she would fuss about the pigtails I made her wear or dresses I chose for her, but we got through it. I know she would have rather worn pants to school, since all the other girls were wearing them at recess. I was still a little old-school though and knew that dresses were what the girls wore when I was growing up. If it was good back then, surely it should be good now.

We made time for Sunday outings, and there were school sports and events that I would continue to attend with the kids, just as I had done before the divorce. It was my intention to maintain a structure and balance in our lives as much as possible.

But by the end of the first year, the demands of the job were beginning to wear on me, and I knew I would have to make some conscious decisions about our family life. Keeping up with the demands of my work and managing my obligation to my family became overwhelming, and as a consequence it forced me to do what I really didn't want to do. I approached my children's mother for help. It was only logical since she still was working in Atlanta, and lived in an apartment not far away from our home. She agreed with this arrangement, and once again, I would find my life in the process of change.

The lives of some people don't change very much, and then there are some, like me, who find themselves in the midst of change every time they turn around. After many changes, you come to realize that change happens, and somehow it all works out for the good, just as the Bible says: Romans 8:28

"*All things work together for good to them that love the Lord and are called according to His purpose and plan...*"

My Sister's Passing

Life is not easy, and there are times when you wonder when all the drama will end. With my sister, it had been a long journey. She had been sick for years, on dialysis for failed kidneys from the progressive disease of diabetes. My mother and I had been her real support. Even when I was still married, I would find the time to leave work three days a week and transport my sister downtown to receive her dialysis treatments. We would make a regular stop at the Varsity Restaurant, known for its delightfully greasy chili dogs and fries, shakes, and burgers. She loved them all, and I did too. It was good to spend the time with her; she was so funny and would try to make light of her circumstances. But with the years on dialysis, her immune system had become weaker, she had lost interest in taking care of herself, and she moved in with my mother.

By now, my mother was aging, and alone, her second husband of twenty years, Otis Allison had passed, but she was strong enough to care for her daughter. As time wore on, even with my limited help, the role of a caregiver took its toll on my mother. My sister had grown children, but their support was meager. Ann eventually contracted gangrene in her foot, and her leg had to be amputated. After the surgery, Ann made jokes about her leg being removed. The doctor had said there was no guarantee that all the infection was gone. Ann seemed so alive coming from the recovery room, but within three days, the gangrene had spread throughout her body and Ann passed away.

Her funeral was so sad; I wondered how Momma would cope. For me, I knew life had to go on.

The Great American Water Company

While still with the Hawks, business opportunities presented themselves, and I eagerly responded. I was approached to do business in bottled water. I acquired a business partner who was a representative for Winn Dixie, a grocery store chain in the south. The Great American Water Company was established. One of our first contracts was with FEMA. There was a flood in Albany, Georgia, where Albany State College had been underwater. We were given the contract to ship our water to the region. Then our largest contract came when a hurricane hit Puerto Rico and we had to ship water to them. Doing well with this gave us the leverage for growth. We set our sights on the 1996 Olympics in Atlanta. What a great moneymaker to have water stations throughout the Olympic area, and I had come up with a great design for our bottle. It was a unique design featuring a picture and write-up of great athletes visible through a peek-a-boo label on the bottle. We needed to secure water that was of high quality and fairly priced, and after searching high and low, we found our water in Canada. Then our bottles had to be manufactured to our specifications. All this was a process and an education for me, an experience that would years later land me in Africa with the vision of establishing a water business there.

During 1996, I was overloaded with life. Hurting from my neck and back injuries, I faced surgery; and with a third divorce, I faced emotional pain. My first surgery, which was for my neck, was on Valentine's Day, and the second for my lower back came May 13 of the same year. My first surgery was stressful to say the least. My daughter thought I shouldn't be alone at home, so she went out and got me a little kitten, and we named her Luckey. Luckey was a comfort to me lying on the bed by my side while I moaned and groaned from the discomfort of the surgery. She was a great addition to my recovery and became a longtime family pet, lasting over fourteen years. Momma also was a great help cooking and cleaning for me.

I had no outside help, and even though I was supposed to be using the time to recover, I was still attending to the business. I was in the hospital and had left my business partner in charge of the day-to-day operations. Decisions needed to be made on how much water to order for our Olympics project. You know, some things are better taken care of by one's self, and that is what I found out when he did not consult me but rather ordered the water himself. Overstocking almost killed us. We had far too many truckloads of water. To make matters worse, the Olympic committee had changed the direction of the route and closed off many streets to the vendors who, by the way, had put their life's savings and mortgaged their homes to create wealth off this Olympics. We were all in trouble. Many of the stations that we had geared up for were now unavailable to us. I was hot, as hot as could be. I had been out of the hospital only a few weeks prior to the Olympics, and instead of resting and recuperating, I was working my tail off to save our business.

My good friends and family members came to help us with the distribution of the water at the Olympics. William Hawkins, Charlie Green, my daughters, son, and other family and friends came out to help. For them and their tireless work, I am ever grateful. We did not sell what we projected, but there was a lot of water left over that we had to sell quickly. Right after the Olympics, we found a buyer at cost and moved the water out. I also was faced with a decision of should I continue to stay in business or get out. I chose the latter, and to this day, I am thankful once again to Attorney Bill Temple, who helped me walk away from the Great American Water Company without any bills and a small amount of change in my pocket.

Atlanta Hosts 1996 Olympics

For me, the summer Olympics was bittersweet. It was a great honor to host the Olympics in my hometown, but how poorly the event was planned. After participating in two Olympics and seeing other Olympics around the world, this one proved to be somewhat of an embarrassment to the Olympic community, and to me. Not to mention how disrespectfully the Georgia Olympians were treated.

When I first heard Atlanta won the bid, I immediately offered my services to the planning committee. There are several Georgia Olympians who came together as a group, hoping to help make an impact in the community for the good. We were organized and had taken the steps to incorporate. It was our vision that our group of professional athletes would go into the schools to educate and motivate the youth with excitement about this great event. A meeting was scheduled with two of the head Olympic staff members and three Olympians. Our goal was to get their blessings on going into the schools and corporations with our gold medals and letting the youth get a glimpse of what it was like to be an Olympian. What a disappointment the meeting turned out to be. Our enthusiasm was met with an apathetic response.

We were offended. If they only knew what it took to be an Olympian, how hard we trained to just make the team, and what an honor it was to represent our country, but they didn't get it. It was all about money and greed. What was so disheartening was the fact that they picked Olympians from other states to work with the Georgia Olympic Committee, and Georgia has some of the greatest athletes who also have gold medals. I say shame on the organizing committee.

I did carry the Olympic torch for three blocks. Being picked early in the planning stages, I didn't know that I would have to go in for surgery. So when they performed the May 13 surgery, immediately during my physical therapy, I would have to prepare my body to carry the torch. The therapist made me a made-up torch for height and weight and taught me how to hold and carry it without hurting my back and neck. Instead of running, I would have to walk, and when it came time for opening ceremonies, I would start the whole event off from the city hall. It was a great honor to be picked despite all the other things that had gone wrong.

The great day came, and after walking those three blocks I was exhausted. I had thought that since we the torchbearers had done our part in carrying the torch, surely we would have a seat at the opening ceremony event inside the stadium. Wrong! When one of the oldest Olympians (he had to be about eighty years old) who had also carried the torch asked one of the Olympic representatives, "What do we do once we finish running the torch?" The reply back was, "If you haven't bought a ticket, you may as well go home." Go home, no ticket—what was that all about? How could anyone say that to an Olympian! Not to have a seat, and here I had run as an Olympian, received a gold medal, represented my country, and then they hadn't any seat, not just for me but for the other Olympians as well! Why? I would ask myself that question for years to come. We were all excluded, but for me, this was a slap in the face. This was my hometown, and I was a decorated Vietnam War hero. No one can imagine the hurt.

I have always been my own man and was taught to be so as a child. That will never change, and part of being my own man is speaking my mind in hopes that I am telling the truth without tainting it through human emotion. I do apologize if through my storytelling I have offended anyone; it clearly has not been my intention. I am a man that will tell you as I see it right or wrong is not the issue. I am not racist or prejudice, and I can be angry at you one minute and turn around to be friends with you the next. That's just me, and I'm not perfect, just forgiven. So to say that the 1996 Olympic experience was good would be a lie. On the whole, it was the most disappointing and hurtful experience that I have encountered in my professional sports career. I am still getting over this one, so now I'll move on.

Daddy Comes Back into My Life

Before the 1996 Olympics, I went to see about my father in Chicago. I guess going through the major health issues I was facing with my neck and back gave me a longing to see my father and spend time with him. He was now aging, and I knew it. When I went there, I found him still living in the same little apartment he had lived for much of his life there. His wife had passed away, leaving him alone to care for himself. His furniture was broken down and his place unkempt. When I was back in Atlanta, my dad's sister, Velmarie, had phoned me about her concerns for him. She said he was drinking a lot and not taking care of himself. Seeing for myself how his conditions were, I immediately went into searching for a different place for him to live. Going over to where his sister lived, I was hoping to find him a place there, but there was no room. I put his name on their waiting list and returned to Atlanta. He may have been out of sight, but he wasn't out of my mind. I would call back periodically with my concerns, and there was no good report. In 1996 after the Olympics was over and my house was now empty, I got a call that Daddy had burned down his little place. I went back to find him since family didn't know where he was. The windows of his place had all been broken out, and it was cold inside and uninhabitable. Going to the landlord, I found that Daddy had been staying there since the fire, but the landlord got him a temporary place with a lady friend.

He gave me the directions, and when I showed up there, Daddy was really surprised.

"Boy, how did you find me?" were his first words.

My heart told me he would have to come home with me. He was in need, and I couldn't turn my back on him and walk away. I would have to do what I knew was right—take care of my dad. So, with his consent, he came home to live with me.

I loved my dad and had never really spent any kind of time during my adult life with him, so the idea of him living with me was great. Sometimes what you think is not always the truth, and when we got home, it was so much different than I thought it would be. My environment was just too quiet for him. I lived outside the city in the suburbs where there wasn't any action, and he needed action. Every time I would turn around, Daddy had left and gone to Dalton. I guess he thought Dalton would be the same as when he left it years ago, but it wasn't. He would go there to look for his old running partners, only to find that most had passed and only a few relatives remained, but they too had grown old. He was also showing signs of dementia, and that became harder to deal with. Daddy had such a winning personality and could make you laugh. Black barbershops have such great camaraderie, and Daddy knew just where to find one. He would leave the house, go down to the barbershop, and entertain them all day. They in turn would give him liquor. He would get drunk, come home, and leave water running. One time I came home to the tub overflown and water leaking through my family room ceiling. This was hard on me since I had a showcase home, and with my dad there, caring for the home became increasingly hard. I had a wet bar in the basement, and one day discovered that Daddy had drunk most of the liquor only to replace the bottles with water. He broke things and let my cat out, I had to go find her, and she was all scratched up. We went to the vet, and that became an additional worry and expense. Daddy said that cats should be outdoors and that became the end of Luckey as an inside cat. Since she now had a taste of the great outdoors, it was hard to keep her in. She seemed to find her way outside every chance she could with the help of Daddy. Oh my! It was clear that Daddy needed more help than I could give him. Since he was a veteran, I approached the VA for help. Although I felt guilty on the one hand, on the other I felt relief. By the year 1997, Daddy was in a new facility, and I was now officially retired from the Hawks.

Asked: I Tried to Serve, Politically

My next adventure was political. In 1997, I was approached by some people in the Georgia Democratic Party asking me to run for the state senate seat. *Run* was a great term, since I knew how to do that. I had always wanted to make my voice heard in the political arena, and now came my opportunity. My time was free since I had found a home for Daddy, was retired from the Hawks, and was in pretty good health. So, after some thought, I stepped into the race. The problem was that I had stepped into the race so late, and as it would have it at election, I found myself coming in third place. Not bad for a latecomer, I thought, but it was obviously too much work, and that was enough of politics for me. I sometimes toy with the idea of running again, but that is as far as it goes.

Not long after my political adventure, I was hired by the DeKalb County Visitors and Convention Bureau as a consultant. My primary job was to bring sporting events into the county. While working with them, I had the opportunity to put on the largest international track and field program in the Atlanta area. Over two thousand athletes came from all over United States and the Caribbean Islands for a week full of events. This event took me close to eight months to develop, and when the event was over, I was done. I went back into my retirement and playing golf.

Momma Comes Home

Now that I had gotten my father settled down and my political venture out of the way, my focus shifted back to Momma. She was in her early eighties and was showing signs of slowing down. I knew that she shouldn't be living alone and that her house would require more than we needed to put into it, not to mention that her neighborhood was changing. I had owned a rental property near Momma and decided to sell it since the market was good. My hopes and intentions were that I could persuade my mother to sell her home too. My home in Stone Mountain was obviously too big for just me, and downsizing was the only way to go. Momma and I could get out of what we had and then go in together on a smaller home, which would be ideal for the both of us. I had no intentions then of marrying again, and so it would just be the two of us.

Well, Momma took forever to make up her mind. Momma was a very independent woman who has always been in charge. My home sold quickly, and I signed a year's lease on a two-bedroom apartment. This should buy me enough time to find just what I was looking for the two of us.

One day I was playing golf with a real estate agent; I learned some valuable insight regarding the value of the properties in Momma's community. He told me that people were selling their homes far below their actual value. When I found out about what had been taking place, I held Momma back from selling until she got the right price. I ended up buying a house and stayed there close to three years before Momma finally sold her home and came to stay. It was 2004; she was about eighty-six years old and still moving around quite well. There were some adjustments to be made since Momma was quite bossy. Since she was used to being independent, it was difficult for her to have someone take care of her. She was a great help though since that year, I would find myself with major health issues that I would have to overcome.

Cancer Comes to My House

Cancer is something I never really thought I would get. When I was diagnosed with prostate cancer; the doctor had said that it most certainly had come from Agent Orange, a name coined for a chemical used to kill foliage in the jungles of Vietnam. Along with prostate cancer, the doctors would soon discover that I had CLL, a slow-growing leukemia. Momma stayed by my side through the six weeks of radiation and chemotherapy treatments. She cooked and cleaned for me and was such a great support. She really kept me encouraged when I fell to my lowest point. It was not easy but with Momma and God's help I made it through.

Surprise, Surprise!

Debbie and Melvin
at Atlanta Sports Hall of Fame Induction

You know how you say you'll never do something again and at that time you think you really mean it? Well, I said I would never marry again, and that was what I had come to believe. I dated for a while after my last divorce and spent time out on the social scene, but after a while, it got tiring. When Momma came to live with me, that was it—no more dating. I would watch movies to fill my time. I had been in church for some years but had not really found the place where I could call a church home. So, you might say I was a church-hopper like so many others. I guess what I was looking for could not be found in church but rather found in me.

Eventually, I made a commitment to myself that I would become more involved with church and God, and so I did. I attended the Providence Missionary Baptist Church in Atlanta and really enjoyed it, so I decided to become a member. I was there about a year, taking my membership classes when I could, and I was still doing quite a bit of travel for golf when the pastor asked me to speak to the youth. It was that Sunday in December of 2006 and I had just come out of the youth service. My pastor was out in the parking lot speaking to a young man and a woman. Curious, I got in my car and decided to pull up to them to see who he was talking to. The young man approached my car, and I introduced myself to him; next he summoned over the woman to meet me. She stuck her hand in to shake mine and the next thing I couldn't let her go. She had such beautiful eyes, and what a smile. It was God who made that meeting that day, and I knew it.

A week later I would take her out on a date. Four months later, I would ask her to marry me and within one year to the date, December 16, 2007, we were married. Debbie is an ordained minister who loves to help people. She and I are so very much a like it isn't funny. I am happy, and I have never known love like this before. It is the honest truth, and I tell everyone I meet about her and how much I love her. She has helped me with my mother, taking care of her as if she were her own mother. She has helped me through some very trying times with illness, and I always tell her I'd give her the moon if I could. I prayed to God for a woman before I met her and all I can say is that God really does hear and answer prayers. She prayed for me too and mirrors my sentiments exactly about our meeting and marriage. Nothing is by accident, and if you believe, as I always say, it will happen.

Heavy Losses

Melvin Pender Sr.

Evelyn Bell Allison

In January 2010, I again would experience great sadness. My father, ninety-four, passed away. The thoughts flooded me about not having time with him both as a child and as an adult. It would take time before I could heal from his passing. In 2013, I would find myself again in grief as I suffered the loss of my beloved mother at ninety-six. I know that we all will someday leave this world, but it still does not ease the pain. Eventually, I would come to rest with it.

Perhaps the greatest gift that God could give us is the gift of family and knowing that we are not alone here on this earth. I have been blessed to have parents, grandparents, and a sister, children and grandchildren, close friends, and acquaintances. Although many have passed on, they will live in my heart and memories.

Let Your Light Shine

Dream your dreams and live your life. Let God be in charge and don't be afraid of change. Great things can happen to you too. This is my expression of hope to you, whoever you are, wherever you are; it doesn't matter if you're young, old, or in the middle age of life: never, never, never give up on your dreams. God is no respecter of persons, and just when you think things are over, that's when they are just beginning. Look at me. The dreams I dreamed as a child came true. I have made mistakes, taken some falls, but have gotten back up and kept on going. Keep going in your race; don't give up, and don't give in, you'll get there. When I was sixteen, I made a promise to my mother that I would make her proud one day. She came to my Officers Candidate School graduation, the 1968 Olympics, my college graduation, and my induction to the Georgia Sports Hall of fame. What an honor to have her there with me. She worked so hard to raise me and my sister scrubbing floors as a maid and bringing home $15 a week. To make something of my life was the least I could do to honor her. No matter what age you are, you still have the opportunity to make your mother, father, family proud—and most of all, make yourself proud of you. Serve God and serve your country. Love, laugh, and be kind to one another. Be truthful and help others; you will be blessed for what you give from your heart. These are words of wisdom from my grandfather to me when I was a little boy. They stuck with me, and I hope they will stick with you.

One day when you sit down to write your story, let it be your *expression of hope* to someone else.

"Love never gives up, never loses faith, is always hopeful, and endures through every circumstance" (1 Cor. 13: 7)

The End

Family Comments

I did not travel with my daddy, but when he was home, we would hang out together, that's the way life is for those of us who are military brats, and we have parents in the military who often are assigned from one military base to another. The moves sometimes produced very good memories. I still remember the joy of going to Vick's Drive In, when my dad was stationed in Fayetteville, North Carolina. Once my dad became more involved in track, it was fun visiting the different college campuses. I like hanging out with my dad, and still do.

Once I started going with Dad to track meets and started seeing him work with young people I knew, he knew, something many others did not, when it came to track. He worked with track programs in the DeKalb County school district, located in suburban Atlanta. He was coordinating the largest track and field meets in DeKalb County's history, the Youth Games Track and Field Invitational Championships. The event was focused on the personal health and fitness of area young people eighteen and under.

When I was six or seven, in California, I got a chance to meet some of the track stars that others dream about: John Carlos, Ralph Boston, Jim Hines, and Bob Hayes, to name a few. Later on, I met and interacted with sprinters Wilma Rudolph and Wyomia Tyus while I was a student at Fisk University. All my friends were as excited about my dad as I was. However, it was not until I was twelve or thirteen, in Manhattan, Kansas, that I began to realize how much my dad had accomplished, and he was a hero to me!

When Dad was an assistant track coach at the West Point Military Academy, I was in high school nearby in Highland Falls, and our graduating class was the first to ever use West Point's Thayer Hall for our high school graduating ceremonies. Germain "Jobie" Pender Stanley is a retired medical billing clerk. She has one daughter, Mia, and granddaughter, Winter.

* * *

Once I started asking questions of my dad, I think I was about eight at the time, I realized how important he has been in American society. There were all these medals all over the house and pictures on the walls and stored up in boxes. He started telling me stories about track and the military and life in America, and I listened. I started paying attention. There were things he told me that he emphasized over and over. They were all about how to succeed, especially as a man growing up black in America. At a very early age, I remember he instilled in me that if you find yourself working as a floor sweeper, you've got to sweep it better than anyone else who had the job. You should never let anyone outwork you in any endeavor, he stressed. And on a job, he emphasized that you should not let anyone outwork you. When readers see the challenges my father faced and made his way through them, they are going to come away knowing they have met someone who not only witnessed some of the most critical history in America, but he was part of it. He has witnessed some of the biggest events of his generation. They will see a lot of America's history through a man's life and through the eyes of someone who was there. My father's athletic accomplishments are unsurpassed. He became a competitive sprinter late in life. He was so fast at the start of a race; starters often thought he had jumped the gun. If he had started running in college back then with the coaching sprinters have now, there is no telling what we would be reading about him now. Javier Pender, is a consultant in Maryland. He is married. He and his wife, Ceriese, have two sons, Rajah and Malachi.

* * *

Growing up I always appreciated and was proud of my father's accomplishments. I watched as many struggled to fully comprehend his continuous achievements and success. Many would say it was luck and only a few actually embraced his true identity.

As I got older, I realized my father's age at which he began his athletic career was a topic frequently discussed. Time after time, sports journalists often found it perplexing as to how my father's age had nothing to do with the world records he was setting. Well before the controversial issue of doping in sports, many had no other words to describe my father's fortitude and how it led to such success, especially since he was competing against others who were much younger.

You see, when I think about my father's life, I never saw him using time or age as an excuse to abandon his dreams. There were no excuses and absolutely no one was going to tell him he couldn't do something. "Now" was always the time to pursue his dreams and overcome any challenge put in his way. No one was going to tell my father "no," and if they did, he fought harder.

What my father possesses is a resolve that comes from God. How do I know this? Because only that kind of a holy resolve breaks chains, sets records, makes history, and steamrolls every test and trial. Above all, because my father's heart has always been in the right place and God continues to use it for many to see the glory of who He is and what He can accomplish through you.

This is what I take away from my father's legacy. Melania resides in Columbia, Maryland, and is currently working on the development of a not-for-profit organization.

About the Author

Dr. Melvin Pender Jr. Biography

"To whom much is given, much is required." Mel Pender has spent many years making this motto a part of his lifestyle by giving back to his community. A native of Atlanta, a retired military officer, Olympian, entrepreneur, and community leader, Mel has made numerous contributions to his community. The construction of the first black pool in Lynwood Park the community, where he grew up, was one of his first contributions; however, motivating youth is his passion and most significant contribution. His professional and life experiences provide the support from which he drafts his message when addressing young audiences. His aim is to inspire and motivate youth to achieve their goals and to remember that once success is achieved they must reach back and help another child succeed.

Entering the US Army at the age of seventeen as an enlisted man, he served eleven years then attended Officers Candidate School where he became an officer. He served in the 9th Division, the Central Intelligence Agency, and as a commanding officer in the 82nd Airborne Division. Captain Pender was assigned two tours in Vietnam, and after serving twenty-one years in the military, he retired in 1976. Among numerous medals and badges, the most distinguished awards were the Bronze Star, the Vietnam Service Medal, the Combat Infantry badge, the Meritorious Service Medal, and the Joint Service commendation medal.

At age twenty-five while playing football on the army team, he discovered his natural talent was track and field. His career as a world-class athlete began while still maintaining his position in the military. To date, Mel holds the world record in the 50- and 60-yard dash. He once held world records in the 70- and 100-yard dash and the 100-meter dash. In 1964, at the age of twenty-seven, he competed in the 1964 Olympics in Tokyo. Mel was pulled out of combat in Vietnam to compete in the 1968 Olympics in Mexico City where he won the gold medal in the 4 x 100-meter relay (at thirty-one, he was the oldest sprinter to compete in the 100 meters relay). He was pulled again from Vietnam for the 1972 Olympic trials; injuring himself, he didn't make the team. Following his Olympic endeavor, Mel was offered several professional football contracts but turned them down to continue his military career.

From 1970 to 1976, he served his last six years at West Point Military Academy as the first black coach of track and field. During 1972 to 1975, while coaching at West Point, Mel worked very hard to complete his education, traveling over one hundred miles daily to Adelphi University. In 1976, Mel earned a BA degree in social science with honors and ran professional track for the International Track

Association concurrently. He set the world record in the 60-yard dash at the age of thirty-five at the time of 5.8 seconds.

After a successful career in sports administration and management, Mel formed his own company, Metro Industries Group, in 1978, a consulting organization as well as the Great American Water Inc., which he later sold. During 1979–1990s, Mel worked for the National Association of Homebuilders as the national coordinator for the Manpower training program of Job Corps. Under his leadership, the Manpower Training Development Division placed first out of six regions, for seven years, in training and placement of job corps members. In 1991, Mel received the highest leadership award, Hands-On Award, for training and job placement of at-risk youth.

In 1990–1996 as director of community affairs for the Atlanta Hawks and president of the Atlanta Hawks Foundation, Mel maintained the organization's visibility in the community while working with government agencies on community programs. He was the Hawks' representative at community functions and coordinated special events and fund-raising activities. Mel also worked as the athletic administrator for the NFL Players Association youth development program.

In 1995, he founded the Gathering of Eagles Foundation and took on the mission to "teach a child how to sew into the fabric of the future." He promotes annual golf tournaments, auctions, and various other special events to raise funds to provide scholarships for young women and men who aspire to go to college.

Dr. Pender served on the board of directors of the United States Sports Academy, the Sickle Cell Foundation, the Inner-City Games, and the Hank Aaron Rookie League. His past board memberships include Southwest Hospital, the Atlanta Chapter of the United Way, Policy Advisory board Of the Atlanta Project and also served as the vice president of the USA Track and Field Association of Georgia in 2001. Always committed to children; he supports the Boys and Girls Clubs of America and has served on the Special Olympics Committee in Georgia. In addition, Mel was an active member of the 100 Black Men Club of DeKalb County

In 2001, Mel initiated and coordinated one of Georgia's largest Youth Games Track and Field Invitational Championships held in DeKalb County, providing top quality amateur competition and promoting physical fitness with personal health training to children ages seven to eighteen. Through the years, he has also coordinated summer camps in track and field skills.

Mel and wife, Rev. Debbie Pender, have formed the M&D Consulting Firm, which provides the service of motivational speaking to the corporate world and young leaders of tomorrow with an inspirational message that "Dreams can come true."

Mel's accomplishments include the following:

- 1964 and 1968 All-American Amateur Athletic Union Award
- 1966 United States Army Infantry Officers School
- 1976 National Black Sports Foundation Hall of Fame Inductee
- 1981 member of Georgia's Criminal Justice Coordinating Council
- 1982 appointed by Gov. George Busbee to the Jail/Prison Overcrowding Committee
- 1984 and 1985 100 % Wrong Club Hall of Fame Inductee
- 1984 Georgia State Sport Hall of Fame Inductee
- 1994 recognized by Dollars and Sense magazine as one of the best and brightest business and professional men
- 1995 US Dept. of Justice Bureau of Investigations / FBI Community Leadership Award
- 1996 Adelphi University Hall of Fame Inductee
- 1995 Awarded the Mel Pender Day by the Mayor of Atlanta (Maynard Jackson)
- 1995 and 1696 Southern Bell Calendar Spirit Legends Award
- 1996 Atlanta Committee for the Youth Advisory Council US Olympic Games
- 1996 Bellsouth Spirit of Legends Hall of Fame Inductee

- 1997 Doctoral Degree from Adelphi University
- 1998 graduated from Leadership Atlanta
- 2001 Bob Hayes Hall of Fame Inductee
- 2006 appointed to the United States Olympic Alumni Board
- 2007 Awarded Mel Pender Day by Vernon Jones CEO of Dekalb Co., Georgia
- 2002 to Present United States Sports Academy
- 2012 Atlanta Sports Hall of Fame Inductee
- 2014 Smyrna Community Steering Committee
- 2015 United States Army Officer Candidate School Hall of Fame Inductee
- 2015 Campaign Chairman for Mayor of Smyrna, Georgia
- 2016 Military Veterans Hall of Fame Inductee

CPSIA information can be obtained
at www.ICGtesting.com
Printed in the USA
FSOW03n1641280217
31373FS